100 AMAZING COMPUTER TIPS

**Shortcuts, tricks, and advice to help everyone
from novice to professional**

Diane McKeever, CPP

Certified Patient Person

SWAN MEDIA

100 Amazing Computer Tips

Published by
Swan Media LLC
303 Sea Anchor Road
Osprey, FLorida 33429
Copyright © 2014 by Swan Media LLC, Osprey, Florida

ISBN 978-1-940745-81-7 (eBook)
ISBN 978-1-940745-82-4 (paperback)

2014.04.19

Printed in the United States of America
10 9 8 7 6 5 4 3 2 1

About the Author

Diane McKeever is a freelance software trainer/ computer coach living in Osprey, Florida. For over twenty-five years she has provided computer guidance to more than 100,000 students at companies such as GTE, Gartner Group, GE and Aetna as well as working with individuals in their homes and small offices. She is as comfortable working with beginner users as she is with advanced professionals. She supports both the PC and Apple environments. Her work has earned her the title, Certified Patient Person, as she has been called by countless students over the years.

More recently she has expanded her business and become certified as a Social Media Marketing Professional. She has lectured extensively to SCORE and Chamber of Commerce groups on the subject and has helped hundreds of businesses set up and use the power of advertising available through social media. Her energetic informative presentations will liven up your organization's next meeting.

Her extraordinary work has garnered her good press and she was featured on the TV program "Extraordinary Women Leading Extraordinary Lives".

Contact Diane (diane@dianemckeever.com) for your training or social media marketing needs.

Introduction

The tips in this book were originally posted to my blog, <u>100 Computer Tips in 100 Days</u>, and were presented there in no particular order. For this book I reorganized them, expanded on many of the entries and added links to other media. I also included some tip cards that I have distributed to participants in my classes. These tip cards have proven to be very popular.

I have had the opportunity over the last twenty-five plus years to work with people with a wide range of computer skill levels. I am often reminded that those things that are "obvious" to me are not at all obvious to everyone else. I laugh every time someone asks, "Now how would I know that?" The computer world has its own language, a language many of us didn't learn in school.

Most of the tips in this book are for both the PC and the Apple environments. However, there may be different keys, such as Ctrl in PC versus Command in Apple used to perform the tips. Differences in Apple will be noted in parenthesis.

This book is not intended to be read from start to finish in one sitting. Many of the techniques should be practiced before you go onto the next tip. Thumb through the book and dip in when you see an interesting topic or start at the beginning and make your way straight through it. Either way, I hope you enjoy the tips I have put together. Give them a try and I am confident that they will save you time and effort every day.

CONTENTS

Internet Browser Tips

Facebook Tips

General Microsoft Office Tips

General Email Tips

Microsoft Outlook

Microsoft Excel Tips

Microsoft Word Tips

Fun Projects & Programs & Other Stuff

Appendices

Quick Reference Guides

GENERAL COMPUTER TIPS

TIP #1 - BASIC MOUSE TERMS

Before we get into the great tips to come, I think it's important to define some terms that you might think are basic but that other people find confusing. Click and Drag are basic mouse actions; Cut, Copy and Paste are actions that you use within programs as well as in folders.

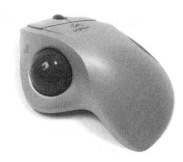

Click – This means to press the mouse button down and then release it quickly. You'll sometimes need to double click, which means to press twice in rapid succession. It's important that when you double click the clicks be close together and that the mouse does not move while you're clicking. If you have problems keeping your mouse steady when you click or double click, you might consider using a different type of mouse, the kind called a track ball. With a track ball the mouse does not move on your desk. Instead, you roll the ball -- as if you are using a mouse upside down.

Examples of trackball mice.

Drag – You use this action to move items from one place to another. To drag something you first place your mouse on the item, hold down the left mouse button and move your mouse on the desk or mouse pad. If you run out of room while you're dragging, simply lift up your mouse while keeping the button pressed down, reposition the mouse on your desk and start dragging again. Of course if you're using a laptop this is easy to do, all you have to do is lift up your finger and start again in a different place.

Copy – When you copy something you leave the original information in place while you put a duplicate of it on the Clipboard. The Clipboard is the computer's holding area for information that was copied or cut and is waiting to be pasted. Because the Clipboard generally only holds one piece of information -- the last thing that you copy or cut -- you should paste right after you copy or cut to avoid losing the information.

Cut – Cut is the same as Copy except the information is removed from its original location. As with Copy, you should paste right after you cut so that the information is not lost.

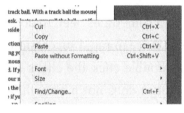

Paste – When you Paste you place the contents of the Clipboard in your document. If Paste is not available then there is no information on the Clipboard and you should Copy or Cut again.

The easiest way to Cut, Copy and Paste is to click with the right mouse button (Ctrl + click on an Apple) once you have selected the item.

Tip #2 - Zooming Windows

Have you ever gone to a website and found that the images and words on the page were way too small to read? If you find that happening to you all of the time you might want to visit the eye doctor but, if it happens only occasionally, you may only need to zoom in on the window. While the zoom command is probably someplace in your program, here is a simple mouse and keyboard combination that can help.

While holding down the Ctrl key roll the wheel of the mouse away from you to zoom in. Made it too large? Use the Ctrl key and roll the wheel of the mouse towards you. Brilliant! What's that, you say, you don't have a wheel on your mouse? Trot on down to your nearest office supply store and get a new mouse. A mouse without a wheel is ready for the retirement village anyway.

Keep in mind that this works not only on a browser window but with just about ANY window. If you are in Word or Excel and want to make that screen larger use Ctrl and the mouse wheel.

This generally works on the Apple while holding down the Command key. The Apple also uses Alt + Command and the plus (+) or minus (-) key to increase or decrease the zoom.

TIP #3 - SAVE VERSUS SAVE AS

In every class I have ever taught, when we save a document I wait for the one person who will ask, "When do I use Save rather than Save As?" The answer is surprisingly simple.

When you are ready to save your document for the first time, many people believe that they need to use Save As in order to name it. The truth is that it doesn't matter which you choose, Save or Save As, for the first save because you will be presented with the same Save As dialog box in either case. You then give your document a name, make sure it's going into the correct folder, and then you click the Save button.

From then on as you work in your document you can click on Save to update the file. Every time you click on Save, the additional changes you make to your document are stored and any previous versions are written over.

The only time you need to use Save As is if you have a document that you want to use to make a different version of the original document. For example, if you are the secretary for an organization and you created a document for the September Minutes and now it is time for you to create an October Minutes document, you can open the September Minutes document, choose Save As from the File menu (or use the File tab in Office 2010), and name the document October Minutes. The original September Minutes document closes and is replaced on your screen with one called October Minutes.

Using Save As saved you time because you have the basic structure of the document from last month to which you simply make changes. You continue working on that document, saving your changes along the way.

You should view Save As as a way to duplicate a document to save you the time and hassle of creating a document from scratch.

TIP #4 - GROWING/SHRINKING FONT SIZE
WITH THE KEYBOARD

This tip works in most word processing programs such as Word, Publisher, PowerPoint or even your email program. It works on both the PC and Apple computers and is really easy to learn.

First you need to type some text and then select the text you want to make larger or smaller. On your keyboard find the following keys - Shift, Ctrl (Command for Apple) and the Greater Than key (>) or the Less Than key (<). Are you getting an idea of where we're going yet?

With the text selected hold down the Shift and Ctrl (Command) keys at the same time. With the two keys de-pressed, strike the Greater Than key to make text larger and the Less Than key to make the text smaller. That's it. The size increments are the same choices you would nor-mally see on the font size selection box (8, 10, 11, 12, 14, 16, 18, etc.) The reason this is pretty cool is that you may not always have access to choose a new font size in pro-grams since there are times the menus are not available. In those cases, you can always use this keyboard option. Give it a try.

8

Tip #5 - Stopping a Runaway Printer

How often have you accidentally sent a document, in its 100 page entirety, to the printer when you only wanted to print page 6? It makes for a great comedic moment but it can be very frustrating. Here's one method you can use to deal with this problem.

Step 1

Remove any paper in the paper intake area. Depending on the printer you may be able to accomplish this by taking out the paper cassette or you can just reach in and grab the whole paper stack. This will, at the very least, give you some time to consider your other options.

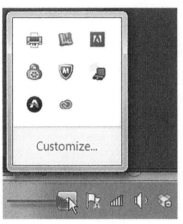

Step 2

Look in the lower right side of your monitor, in the tray area. You should see a little printer icon. You may have to click on "show hidden icons" to see the printer. When it appears in the tray area, double click it.

You will see the printer dialog box. This is good because you will be able to cancel the print job. From the Printer menu choose "Cancel all documents". You'll be asked to confirm this action.

You may have to restart your computer as well as the printer to remove the document from the print spooler queue.

Step 3

Turn everything back on, put the paper back in the printer and all should be good. If not, repeat the steps.

TIP #6 - DUPLICATING WITH THE CTRL KEY

One of the great things about having one company, like Microsoft, dominate the software environment is that there is a lot of consistency in its many programs. An example of that is the ability to Ctrl + mouse drag (hold down the Ctrl key, hold down the mouse button and drag) to duplicate objects. In this case "objects" can refer to text, calendar events, worksheets or graphic objects. Here are some of the ways I use Ctrl + drag.

Outlook - When I set up an appointment with a new client I put in all kinds of information in the event window such as directions, phone numbers and the like. When I have a second appointment I want to avoid entering that all again so I find a previous appointment, hold down the Ctrl key and drag the appointment to another day. When I release the mouse button the duplicate of the original appointment stays. Now all I have to do is change the date of that duplicated appointment and I'm all set.

Excel - When I want to duplicate a worksheet in Excel, I put my mouse on the sheet tab, in the lower left side of the screen, of the sheet I want to duplicate, hold down the Ctrl key and drag the mouse to the right or left. As you do this you will see a little black triangle indicating where the duplicated sheet will be placed. When you release your mouse button the sheet will have been duplicated. Once the sheet is duplicated you can release the mouse button! This is particularly valuable because it duplicates the sheet as well as any Page Layout settings the sheet had such as orientation, print area, frozen panes, etc.

Word - To duplicate text in a Word document you use the same technique. First, you have to select the text you want to duplicate. Then leave your mouse on the selected text, hold down the Ctrl key and drag the text to a new location. When you drag your mouse in Word you will see a dotted vertical line indicating where the duplicated text will be placed.

PowerPoint or **Publisher** - Here Ctrl + drag really comes in handy. If you've drawn a box, created a line, inserted a picture or clip art, etc., and want to duplicate it, use Ctrl + drag. Click on the object, hold down the Ctrl key, hold down the mouse button and drag. When you release the mouse button you have copied the original object. Imagine if you want to scatter a bunch of stars on the page, rather than copying and pasting and ending up with a pile of the stars in the center of the page, you can use Ctrl + drag to duplicate them all over the page. It's a snap!

Just remember to release the mouse button BEFORE you release the Ctrl key.

Tip #7 - Important Keyboard Shortcuts

Many people resist using keyboard shortcuts because they feel they're hard to remember and they have better things to do with their mind. I certainly agree with this but I feel that there are a few shortcuts that are worth working on because they make you more efficient. And in some cases, they are more than shortcuts because there are times you cannot use menus to accomplish these actions.

Two are very easy to remember because the keyboard shortcut is the same as the first letter of what they do. These are Ctrl + s for Save and Ctrl + p for Print (or Command key in the Apple environment).

In addition to these simple shortcuts I would also encourage you to learn and use four more, undo, cut, copy and paste. These are not going to seem as logical as Print and Save unless you know the thought process behind how they were assigned. If you look at your keyboard (or the picture to the left) you will see that on the bottom row, left side we have Z, X, C and V all in a row. When you use these keys in conjunction with the Ctrl key (remember it's the Command key in the Apple world) you will be able to Undo, Cut, Copy or Paste.

The first time I saw these shortcuts in use was on the keyboard for my first Macintosh in 1984. These keys actually had the words Undo, Cut, Copy and Paste written on them as well as the actual letters, and there are still keyboards that have this. Look carefully at your keyboard, you might be surprised!

To Recap:

Save	Ctrl + s
Print	Ctrl + p
Undo	Ctrl + z
Cut	Ctrl + x
Copy	Ctrl + c
Paste	Ctrl + v

14

Tip #8 - Permanently Deleting Files

I think that most computer users know that they can delete files by dragging them to the recycle bin OR selecting them and pressing the Delete key OR right clicking on them and choosing Delete. But where do they go? They go into the Recycle Bin (Trash Can) and periodically you need to empty that. Let's assume that you have a document that you REALLY didn't want to have on your computer any longer and want to permanently delete it in one action. You can and here's how.

Select the file by clicking on it. Hold down the Shift key and tap the Delete key. A little window will pop up asking if you are REALLY sure you want to PERMANENTLY delete this file. Click Yes if you're really sure you do.

BTW, try this in your Outlook program. It works there too. You can delete emails without sending them to the Trash folder.

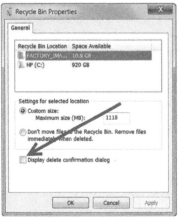

Since we're talking about trash, if you're tired of being asked if you're sure you want to put something in the trash every time you delete something, here's another good tip. Right click on the Recycle Bin and left click on Properties. Uncheck "Display delete confirmation dialog". Now you can delete without that annoying "are you sure" prompt. Whew!

Tip #9 - Using the Right Mouse Button

Those of you who already use the Right Mouse Button (Ctrl + click for you Apple folks) don't have to read any further but I find that many people still do not use this handy feature. This tip is for them.

Right Mouse Button

I once heard a tech support person advising a user to never click on the right mouse button because it would only get them in trouble!!! Nothing could be farther from the truth. The right mouse button actually holds all of the commands in your computer, displaying the correct options available at that moment in time based upon where you are on the screen, or what is selected.

Try typing some text in your favorite word processing program. Select the text and leaving your mouse on the selected text, right click the mouse button. You should see a shortcut menu listing actions you can take such as cut, copy, spell check, etc. Move over to this shortcut menu and make a choice using your LEFT mouse button.

Remember: Only use the right mouse button to see your options, use the left mouse button to choose an option.

This saves a lot of time because you're not checking out a series of menus or tabs to find a particular command; it is right there on the shortcut menu.

18

Tip #10 - More Keyboard Shortcuts

Here are some keyboard shortcuts for those of you who enjoy using your keyboard rather than a mouse. Note that the PC shortcuts use the neglected Windows Key. Striking Windows Key all by itself brings up the Start menu.

Operation	Key combination
Minimize all windows	Windows Key + M
Maximize all windows	Windows Key + Shift + M
Find files on your computer	Windows Key + F
Open My Computer window	Windows Key + E
Open the Run Program Dialog	Windows Key + R

Here are some helpful Apple Keyboard Shortcuts

Operation	Key combination
Open desktop folder	Command-Shift-D
Eject	Command-E
Navigate to the search field in an already-open Spotlight window	Command-Option-F
Open the Home folder of the currently logged-in user account	Command-Shift-H
Go to Folder	Command-Shift-G
Get Info	Command-I
Show View Options	Command-J
Minimize window	Command-M
Minimize all windows	Command-Option-M
New folder	Command-Shift-N
Log Out immediately	Command-Shift-Option-Q
Close all windows	Command-Option-W
Cycle through open Finder windows	Command-Accent (`)*

*Note: The Accent key is above the Tab key on a US English keyboard layout. The next time you're sitting in front of your computer, try these shortcuts out. You may find they're cool.

TIP #11 - SELECTING OBJECTS (FILES, FOLDERS, ETC.)

So often you need to select a group of files to delete, move or copy. It's tedious to do that to individual files. Instead of selecting them individually, use the Shift or Ctrl (Command) keys to select the group.

Selecting consecutive files:

- Click on the first file

- Hold down the Shift key

- Click on the last file you want to select

Selecting non-consecutive files:

- Click on the first file

- Hold down the Ctrl (Command) key

- Click on the other files, one at a time

This tip is a particularly useful one because it also works when you are attaching or opening files or if you're selecting a group of emails to move or delete.

TIP #12 - RESIZING GRAPHICS FROM THE CENTER

You are putting some final touches on your Word, PowerPoint, Publisher, or Excel document and you want to make a graphic or picture a little larger. But because it took you so long to get the picture placed just where you want it vertically and horizontally, you decide to just leave it alone. You know that if you resize it using the corner resize handles then you'll have to spend more time than you really have moving it left, right, up or down to center it again. Not so. What you need to do is resize the picture from the center rather than from a corner.

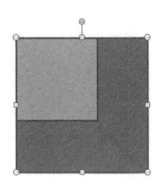

As you probably know, when you select a picture you see resize handles in the four corners as well as half way along each of the four sides. To keep the picture in proportion you should always use the corner handles to resize it. When you do this the two sides that make up the corner you are using become resized. As a result it changes how the picture "sits" in the document.

Here's the way to make the picture stay where you put it originally. Hold down the Ctrl (Alt on the Apple) key while resizing the picture; this will resize it from the center. Those of you who have problems keeping your layout design consistent while resizing pictures will appreciate this tip.

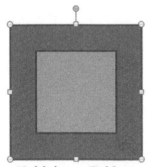

Hold down Ctrl key

TIP #13 - INSERTING A HORIZONTAL LINE

Here's another easy tip that is specific to Word and Outlook. I have tried it in other programs but haven't found any other Microsoft software in which it works.

If you would like to put a nice horizontal line in your document, all you have to do is type three dashes (----) and press the enter key (return in Apple land). The three dashes will be replaced with a single line that goes from the left margin to the right margin. If you change the margins the line resizes automatically.

You can also create a double line, this time with the equal key. Type three equal signs (===) and press the enter key. Voila! You now have a double line that extends from the left margin to the right.

If you need to insert an arrow in your text just type equal, equal and the greater than symbol (==>). This will automatically be converted to this dark arrow. ➜. Want a thinner arrow? Try dash, dash, greater than (-->) and you will get this lighter version of the arrow →

If this doesn't work for you then you might have auto-correct turned off, and why would you do that? Because it's on by default in all Microsoft software, you have turned it off and, therefore, know how to turn it back on. I don't want to give anyone ideas about turning it off.

TIP #14 - QUICK, HIDE ALL YOUR WINDOWS!

Let's suppose you have a ton of windows open and want to quickly see your desktop. You can hide all windows, revealing only what's on the computer's desktop, with one keystroke: hit the Windows key and d simultaneously in Windows, or press F11 on Macs (on recent Mac lap tops, Command+F3).

This tip is great for when the boss or your spouse comes in your office and you're checking your Facebook page or buying a special present for him/her. It's also helpful when you want examine or delete something you've just downloaded to the desktop. Press the keystroke again to reopen all of your windows again.

That's it-- a case of peek-a-boo!

Tip #15 - Double-click the Title Bar and See What Happens

Double clicking the title bar will toggle between "restore down" and Maximize your window in the PC environment. In the Apple environment it will Minimize your window down to the docking area at the bottom right of your screen.

What's the title bar, you ask? It's that area across the top of the window that tells you the name of the window you're looking at. The Title Bar generally includes the close button (Apple) or close X (PC).

This tip always works in the PC environment but might be disabled in the Apple world. If so, go to System Preferences, Dock and click the checkbox for Double-click a window's title bar to minimize.

Tip #16 - Screen Captures

While you were always able to take a screen shot (picture of your screen) by tapping the Print Scr key on your keyboard, it took a picture of your entire screen which you then had to paste into a Word or PowerPoint document to crop it.

Beginning with Windows 7, Microsoft included the Snipping tool. The Snipping tool allows you to take a screen shot of a portion of your screen, helpful if you're trying to show someone what you see on your screen, such as when you're talking to technical support about computer issues.

To access the Snipping tool:

- Click on the Start button or the Windows button in the lower left side of your screen. When you do that your curser will be in the "Search Programs and Files" box.

- Start typing "snip". By the time you get those four characters in the search box you should see the Snipping tool listed in the program menu above.

- Click on the Snipping tool. A window will pop up on your screen with the Snipping tool visible.

- Click the New button to take a picture of an area of the screen. Now drag your mouse on the screen to capture the picture.

- When you release your mouse another window will pop up with your screen capture. You can save it or copy it for use later.

In the Apple environment you can take a screen shot of your entire screen by:

- Hold down the Command and Shift keys and pressing the 3 key.

- You'll hear a camera shutter sound and a new icon will appear on your desktop labeled PictureX.

In the Apple environment you can capture a portion of your screen

- Hold down the Command and Shift keys and press the 4 key,

- Mac OS X turns the cursor into crosshairs. You can use the crosshairs to select whatever portion of your screen you'd like to capture in a screen shot.

Just as in the PC environment, you can paste the screenshot into Word, PowerPoint or email.

TIP #17 - COMPRESSING PHOTOS FOR EMAILING

It is not generally recommended that you attach more than two or three pictures to an email because of the limits on the size of attachments. Of course, you can resize the pictures in programs such as iPhoto or Picasa. Another way is to use the "send to" feature of your operating system, both PC and Apple.

To use the "Send to" feature:

- Find a picture or pictures that you would like to attach to an email and click on it. Remember you can use the Ctrl key to select more than one picture.

- Leave your mouse on one of the selected pictures and click the right mouse button.

- From the pop out menu that appears, select Send to, and click on Mail Recipient.

- A further dialog box will appear from which you can choose the picture size. See the table below from the Kodak website to determine the appropriate file size.

Kodak suggests these resolution/file sizes if the recipient wants to print the attachments:

Print size	Minimum resolution
4" x 6" print	640 x 480 pixels
5" x 7" print	1024 x 768 pixels
8" x 10" print	1536 x 1024 pixels
16" x 20" print	1600 x 1200 pixels
20" x 30" print	1600 x 1200 pixels

Of course, the larger the file size, the fewer files you should attach to the email.

Tip #18 - Improving Computer Speed

The number one complaint I hear about people's computers is that they are running slowly. Of course, your computer will never run as fast as the first day you take it home from the store. Remember how you thought your new computer was faster than the speed of light? Every time you visit a webpage traces of your actions are stored on your computer. These little files add up until your browsing has slowed to a crawl.

Periodically you should run a computer cleaner. For the PC there is a dandy FREE program called CCleaner (originally called Crap Cleaner, I guess they cleaned up their act too!) that is available for download from many sources. Just do a search for CCleaner. I'm particularly comfortable using the cnet.com website for downloading these types of files.

CCleaner is a freeware system optimization, privacy and cleaning tool. It removes unused files from your system, allowing Windows to run faster and freeing up valuable hard disk space.

It also cleans traces of your online activities such as your Internet history. Additionally it contains a fully featured registry cleaner. But the best part is that it's fast, normally taking less than a minute to run, and contains NO Spyware or Adware!

I looked for a free program like CCleaner for the Mac but didn't find a really good one. If you have an Apple you might consider a $39.99 investment in MacKeeper.

The MacKeeper clean-up utilities free up a significant amount of space on your hard drive, doing this quickly and efficiently. As for standalone tools, they take care of your Mac by hiding and encrypting your private files, completely removing the uninstalled apps, recovering accidentally deleted files even if they were removed from the Trash, and more.

And finally, MacKeeper's exclusive online services will help you get answers to any Mac-related questions and even track down your Mac in case it gets stolen. If your Mac is stolen you log in to your MacKeeper account and click the "Mac Was Stolen" button. When the thief opens the computer the built in camera will take a picture of the thief as well as his location and the location of his internet connection. That sounds like a sweet "gotcha" moment.

Tip #19 - Free Anti-Virus Programs

Everyone is concerned about getting a virus on their computer, and they should be. Viruses can be debilitating to your computer and should be avoided at all costs. Speaking of costs, many of these programs cost a lot every year and often do more than you need. Here are two free programs you should consider using on your computer when your current anti-virus program subscription runs out.

If you have an Apple and are sitting reading this thinking you are immune, you should consider downloading the programs too. In the Spring of 2012, more than 600,000 Apples were infected with a trojan from Russia and the conventional wisdom since then is that anti-virus programs are for everyone on every device, phones as well as computers.

Avast Free (www.avast.com) is available for PC and Apple users. Just download it and the software will be installed automatically.

Another alternative is AVG Free (www.avg.com). It is similar to Avast Free but is only available for the PC, although they do have a program for the Mac that will alert you if a website contains malicious threats.

Do not use more than one anti-virus program at a time. If you are currently using Norton Anti-Virus or McAfee Anti-Virus, wait until your subscription runs out and then uninstall that software before you install Avast or AVG.

Better safe than sorry.

TIP #20 - DROPBOX FOR DOCUMENT SHARING OR BACK UP

One of my favorite free programs to store and share documents is Dropbox. It uses cloud technology which allows me to access my files from any computer. This is helpful if you travel without your computer but need to work on files.

To access your files remotely, log on to any computer, bring up a browser and sign into your Dropbox account. Instantly you will see all of the folders and files you have saved in your local Dropbox.

You can also create specific folders in your Dropbox to share with others, which is an important feature if you need to share documents with an individual or a committee.

Who might benefit from using this service? I think almost everyone could. You can use it as an extra storage area for files you don't want to lose. If something happens to your computer, all of the files stored in the Dropbox will be safe and available. If you're a teacher or a member of a committee and need students or coworkers to send you files, create a shared folder and the students can drop their submissions into the special folder.

Get creative and let me know how you're using your Dropbox program.

TIP #21 - LOCK YOUR WINDOWS

Quick, someone is coming, lock your windows! Or maybe you have to dash off and you don't want to close or hide your windows, but you do want to lock your windows so that no one can access your computer in your absence. Well if either of these scenarios sounds good to you then you need to know about Windows + L. I'm referring to the seldom used Windows key, the one with the Windows logo on it.

When you try it you will find it gets you to the sign on screen. If you have added a password to your account your computer will be safe until you return.

If you haven't added a password but would like to add one:

- Click the Start button in the lower left of your screen and choose Control Panel,

- Choose User Accounts and Family Safety.

- Click on User Accounts and then Change Your Windows Password.

- Lastly, click Create a Password for your account. You'll have to type the new password twice. Now when you lock your computer you will have to enter the password to unlock it.

On the Apple you have a couple of ways to go to lock your computer. One way is to activate a padlock that will be displayed on the Right Hand menu bar and the other is to set a hot corner.

If you choose "Show Status in Menu Bar" from Keychain Access, Preferences, General you will get a little padlock in the Right Hand menu bar. This has a menu "Lock Screen, ..." which will automatically switch to the screensaver and require entry of a password to get back (it does allow switching to another user if Fast User Switching is enabled).

The second Apple strategy is to set a "hot corner" for your screen saver so that when you drag your mouse to that corner the screen saver comes on. You also need to set your screen saver so that it requires a password to return to your computer session.

To set up a hot corner on your Apple machine:
- Click the Apple menu in the top-left corner of the screen,

- Select System Preferences, then click the Mission Control icon.

- Click the "Hot Corners" button, and you'll see a new window with four pull-down menus, one for each of your hot corners.

- Select an option for one or all four corners. Among your choices: Mission Control, Application Windows (which highlights all the open windows for the application you're currently using), Desktop (revealing the desktop), Dashboard (which turns on the Mac's panel of "dashboard" widgets), Launchpad (the new iPhone-like launcher for the apps installed on your Mac), Start (or Disable) Screen Saver, and Put Display to Sleep.

Remember that you can choose the same action for two or more hot corners, if you wish. And to keep a corner cold, just choose the "-" option. When you're done, click the OK button.

TIP #22 - CHANGING YOUR DESKTOP PICTURE

Probably the most important thing you need to have is a good desktop picture, one that's appealing to you. Whether it's your dog, child/grandchild, favorite destination or just a plain color, you look at your desktop all the time so it should be a good choice for you. This process couldn't be easier on the PC, and only a little more complicated on the Apple.

Steps to set your Desktop picture on a PC:

- Locate a picture anywhere on your computer you would like to use for your Desktop.

- Click with the right mouse button.

- One of your choices from the menu will be "Set as Desktop Pattern".

When you hide all of the windows you have open (remember windows key + d) you will see your new desktop picture. Remember to choose a picture that is big enough --that it has enough pixels, or the desktop picture will appear dotty.

If you have an Apple follow these steps to change your Desktop picture:

- From the Apple menu, choose System Preferences.

- In the window, click Desktop & Screen Saver, then click the Desktop tab to display just the desktop preferences.

- If you want to use a photo from your iPhoto Library, select Library in the left pane. Otherwise, select Choose Folder, navigate to and select the folder that contains your image, and click Choose.

- In the right pane, click any thumbnail to place the image on the desktop.

- Depending on the size of your chosen image, you can opt to tile or center it if it's small. Note: Your image will look pixelated or have jagged edges if it's too small. Or have the image fill the screen, or stretch to fill the screen. Just choose an item from the pop-up menu that appears above the thumbnails, the one next to the thumbnail of your current picture.

It's so simple you can change the desktop picture daily! Oh yes, some people do.

TIP #23 - WINDOWS AERO SNAP FEATURE

If you have Windows 7 or a later version, you can use Aero Snap to arrange windows side by side, which can be especially helpful when comparing two documents or when moving files from one place to another. With Aero Snap you can grab a window from the Title Bar and move your mouse to the left or right edge of the screen and the window will resize to fill half the screen. Repeat with a second window, this time going to the opposite side of the screen. Now with two easy motions you have a setup that makes both of these screens visible.

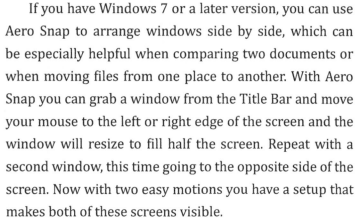

In researching this tip I learned that you can also accomplish this from the keyboard, making it even easier. Click on one of the windows to make it active and from your keyboard hold down the Windows key and press the left arrow key. Now click the other window and use the Windows key and the right arrow key. Shazam! Windows key and the up arrow returns the window to a maximized position.

Apple people have been a little envious about the ability to accomplish this in the Windows environment but it was not part of the Apple OS. You can download a program called "Cinch" from the Apple store (less than $10), which will allow Apple computers to accomplish the same thing.

Tip #24 - Snap To Default Answer

The Snap To feature on your Windows computer automatically moves your mouse to the default answer in a dialog box. It can save you a lot of scrolling around the window when all you want to do is click OK or Save or whatever the blue outlined default answer is. It's particularly helpful for lap tops.

To turn Snap To on:
- Control Panel > Ease of Access > Ease of Access Center > Change How Your Mouse Works.

- Scroll down to the bottom of the window and click Mouse Settings.

- Click the Pointer Options tab and click the checkbox for "Automatically move pointer to the default button in a dialog box".

- Click OK .

Apple users can download a program called Lazy Mouse to accomplish this. Lazy Mouse is free to try and $9.95 to buy.

If you think that's a lot for a product that seems to do one thing, here's a tip for you. Rather than moving your mouse to click on a default answer, you can accomplish the same thing that the software does by pressing the Enter/Return key. The Enter/Return shortcut works on both PC and Apple environments.

Tip #25 - Develop a Backup Strategy

One of the most disturbing days of a computer user's life is the day that his or her computer dies. It's a little known fact that every computer has a surprise expiration date and everyone needs to be prepared for when that day comes. I'm not suggesting that this is a real built-in expiration date but just know that one day your computer will probably die without warning.

There are countless options available from free document back-up to services that will back up the entire hard drive or paid services. All of these are better and more reliable than the external drive sitting next to your computer. This external local backup is popular because people feel it is more secure than using a remote location. But you should understand that commercial remote locations use a series of encryptions that make them extremely safe and secure. The most troubling aspect of local backup is that the backup device is in the same environment as the primary computer. If you get a power surge from a lightning strike it will blow out your computer and the backup. Here are some alternatives.

Microsoft has Skydrive, which offers free cloud-based storage for documents and pictures. There is a fee if you need more than 7GB of storage, but that's a lot of free storage.

Amazon Cloud Drive provides 5GB of free storage. When it was first introduced, you could also use it to stream music. Now that functionality is in a separate service: Amazon Cloud Player. With this latter service, you can upload and stream up to a rather minimal 250 songs to Windows PCs, Macs, and Apple and Android devices.

Apple iCloud comes with 5GB of free storage, but it's more than just storage. Music, apps, books, and TV shows you purchase from the iTunes store, as well as your Photo Stream, can also be stored and streamed from it, and none of the purchased media counts against your sto ota.

Dropbox - See Tip 20 which was devoted to this great free product.

There are also paid services, such as Carbonite (www. carbonite.com) that you might consider. The advantage of these services is that they automatically back up every-thing on your computer without having to store files in special folders as you do with the other services. If your computer dies-- OK when your computer dies -- you buy a new computer, log on to your Carbonite account and click the "Restore" button. All of the files that were on your old computer are transferred to your new computer automat-ically. This is the service that I use and feel it's well worth the $60 a year. They do offer multiple computer discounts.

I don't want to be there when you realize that all of those pictures of your kids, grands or pets just evaporated so, please, do something to back up your documents now.

Tip #26 - Three Finger Salute

The three-finger salute refers to the original PC-compatible system command to reboot or restart a computer by pressing three keys simultaneously: Control, Alt and Delete. The three-key combination is specifically designed to be impossible to execute with one hand in order to avoid the potential for accidental reboots.

When a program freezes or "hangs up" on your computer, you might not want to restart the whole computer but only the one program that isn't responding. Using Ctrl+Alt+Delete will result in a selection of choices that varies by the version of the operating system you're using. One of the choices will be "Start Task Manager".

The Task Manager is a good starting point to identify what programs are running and which might have gotten "stuck". Click on the troublesome program in the list and then click the End Task button. Now you have to be patient. Clicking End Task multiple times does not make the computer respond quicker, in fact just the reverse is true. Multiple clicks slow down the process.

You may get another window saying the program is not responding. Just ignore it. If the program does not end in five minutes, you have my permission to choose Restart from the start button or hold down the power button to turn your computer off.

Ctrl+Alt+Delete is not a keyboard shortcut for anything on the Apple. However, in Mac OS X Server logon screen, pressing Control+ ⌥Option+Delete (the Option key is the equivalent of Alt key on a Mac keyboard) will show an alert saying "This is not DOS." Now who says programmers don't have a sense of humor?

The Apple system does have something compara-
ble to the Task Manager for programs that will not Quit.
⌥Option+⌘Command+Esc will force quit applications.

TIP #27 - FTP VIA SKYPE

Here's a tip for those of you who need to share big files, files too big to attach to an email.

Recently I had to send a BIG graphic file to China for a client but the file was too big to attach to an email. The provider asked if I had a Skype account (of course I did, how else can I see the grands) so we exchanged Skype names.

Sending files via Skype:

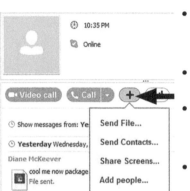

- If necessary, add the individual's name to your contact list.

- Double clicked the person's name,

- Click the plus sign button and choose Send File. That brings up the standard dialog box to choose the file.

- Once the file is chosen then click on the Video call button.

- When the contact accepts the call the download starts automatically. Depending on the file size this process might take a few minutes but you will get a confirmation that the file has been transferred.

In only a few minutes a huge file had been transferred from Florida, USA to Shanghai, China! Isn't the internet a wonderful thing?

Tip #28 - Scrolling Wheel - Scrolling Left and Right and Then Some!

Since the scrolling wheel was introduced to the mouse, scrolling has become so much easier. You don't have to move the mouse over to the scroll bar on the window to go up or down. The scrolling wheel also allows you to scroll horizontally, left or right, but that's not obvious at all.

To activate the left/right feature you have to click the scrolling wheel, that's right, the scrolling wheel is also a button! When you click the scrolling wheel you will see the icon pictured here. Now move your mouse (without clicking anything) just above, below, to the left or to the right of the icon. The further you move away from the icon the faster you scroll, so watch out! To turn off scrolling, click the scrolling wheel again. This button is especially helpful in Excel or webpages that require a left right scroll.

Sorry to say I haven't been able to find anyway to accomplish this on lap tops with track pads or on Apple mice, although Apple's new Magic Mouse allows you to swipe left and right to scroll. I was just reading that the Apple Magic Mouse works on PC's with Windows 7 or 8.

Some other uses of the Scrolling Wheel:

Close Browser Tabs Quickly

I routinely have many tabs open in my browser at any given time. If I want to close a tab, I have to click it, then click the little x that appears on the tab. That's one more click than I prefer, and it makes a tab active that I'm planning to close anyway. Crazy, right?

If you wheel-click any tab in your browser, boom, it's gone. No need to make it active first, no need to click on the "x". Just wheel-click, and, boom, it's closed.

Open Links in a New Tab

When you wheel-click a link in most browsers, that link opens immediately in a new tab rather than changing the content of the current tab. This is especially important when you're comparing items and want to move back and forth between tabs.

Incidentally, you can accomplish the same thing by holding down the Ctrl key and left-clicking a link. But why bother with that when you can just as easily click the middle mouse button?

INTERNET BROWSER TIPS

Tip #29 - Browsing With a URL

When you cruise around on the internet you need to use a browser. There are many browsers available but most people are using one of the following: Internet Explorer, Safari, Google Chrome or Firefox. Internet Explorer comes preloaded on a PC while Safari is the preferred browser for Apple users. You might try a few of these browsers out to see which one has the most comfortable feel to you. Open your browser and type in the browser name to download a copy.

Hypertext
Transfer   World Wide   Unique Domain
Protocol   Web   Name
http://www.dianemckeever.com

Once you open your browser, you need to put in a URL, or Universal Resource Locator, to get to a specific webpage. The URL refers to the unique address of a webpage.

This address is made up of three parts:

- http refers to the language that the webpage was written in. All web pages are written in hypertext markup language or HTML.

- www refers to the world wide web.

- The information that follows www is the unique domain name of the specific page.

When you enter a URL in the address area of the browser it is not necessary to enter the http://www part of the address, as these are implied. If you opened a browser and want to go to Google's site you would type "google" and press the Enter or Return key on the keyboard. In this case the .com is even implied.

If you need to copy and paste a URL, right click on the address area and then choose Copy. Go to your email or wherever you want to insert the URL and right click and choose Paste. If you are pasting the URL into the Browser address area from an email or other source, many browsers now offer you "Paste and Go" as well as the traditional "Paste" as an alternative when you click with the right mouse button.

Now when someone asks what the URL of a website is, you know how to answer.

TIP #30 - USING TABBED BROWSERS

Since 2006, all major web browsers have featured a tabbed interface. More than six years later, many users still do not understand the value of these tabs in a browser.

My computer is on 24-7 and my browser is always open. Using the tabs feature I am able to quickly switch between Google searches, Gmail, FaceBook, my calendar and other frequently used sites.

When you're shopping you can open multiple tabs and compare the prices you've seen on BestBuy versus Amazon versus Staples. If you need another tab opened, click the little new tab on the right side of the tab area. Tabs can be closed selectively by using the close "x" or the entire browser can be closed using the windows close button.

When you use the big "X" to close the browser you will often see a dialog box asking if you want to close the active tab or all of the tabs. You may have seen this dialog box and wondered why it was asking that. Now you know. Notice in this dialog box that you can select the option to stop asking you this question.

A great feature of tabs is that you can set up the option to reopen all of your tabs when you reopen the browser. This makes it easy to go back to what you had opened when you have "unexpectedly" quit from the browser or have to restart your computer and your browser after downloading software.

In Safari browser tabs are restored by default and many people have a problem with that because there is no setting to revise it. However, if you hold down the Shift key while opening Safari it does not restore the last set of tabs.

The reopening settings for this on Chrome is in the "Customize and Control Google Chrome" menu in the upper right corner, while on Firefox it's in the Tools menu, Options area.

Tip #31 - Initiating a Google Search with a Right Click

This is a cool tip that I only learned recently, and I learned it by accident! I selected a word on a webpage and when I right-clicked to copy it I noticed the Search option. When you are in a browser, any browser, and you select a phrase, you can then click with the Right mouse button (Apple users should use Ctrl click). One of the choices you will see in the shortcut menu is to Search Google for "phrase you have selected".

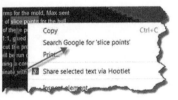

That's it! This tip is short and sweet but one that I think you will use a lot, I know I do.

TIP #32 - GOOGLE MATH

Google is known for its ability to do searches but it can also do math!

Just type an equation in the search box, such as 23*7+15/3=, and press the Enter (Return) key. Not only is the answer displayed but a calculator appears on your screen in case you have to do more equations.

Those of you who use Excel will notice that the equal sign goes at the end of the equation, not at the beginning.

No more hunting for the calculator, just use the Google search screen.

Note: If you are using Google Chrome as your browser you can type the equation in the address bar with the same result.

Tip #33 - Google Translate Tool

Have you ever wanted to write a note to someone using a language other than the one you speak? Google has made it easy for you to accomplish this.

Here's how to use the Google Translate Tool:

- In any web browser type the address: "translate. google.com". You will see two side by side boxes.

- In the left box, type the text using your native language. Google will try to automatically detect the language you are using. As you type the text in the left box, it is being translated in the right box.

- If Google isn't translating it into the correct language, use the To: box to identify the language Google should use for the translation.

- Hover over a word or phrase in the translated text to see alternative suggestions.

- You can even hear your translation by clicking on the speaker below the translated text.

Since my language skills are pretty shaky even in English, I can't vouch for the quality of the translations but they've got to be better than my high school foreign language expertise.

Tip #34 - Refining Your Internet Searches

Are you surprised by some of the results you get when you do an Internet search? The search engines try to identify for you the websites that best fit your search terms. If you were to search for "turkey burgers" your results will include pages that have general turkey recipes as well as information about burgers, not necessarily only burgers made from turkey meat.

To find pages devoted specifically to turkey burgers, enclose the term in quotation marks. This is particularly helpful if you're looking for "John Q Public" or anyone else. By putting quotation marks around their name it will be looking for people with that specific name.

Here are some other, lesser known search modifiers:

- **allintitle:admissions policies** searches for the words admissions policies in the title assigned to the page by the programmer

- **allintext:best museum jobs** searches for the pages using all of the terms

- **allinurl:admissions** searches for the word admissions in the URL

- **define:blog** shows definitions from pages on the web for the term blog

- **related:www.nbc.com** will show similar pages to nbc.com

- **movie:gone with the wind** will find movie-related information for Gone With The Wind

- **minus in your search** removes that word from the page "cats –dogs" results in finding pages that mention cats but not dogs.

Also, don't bother putting "the", "and", "of" and so forth in web searches unless they are part of a longer phrase within quotation marks.

Tip #35 - Copying Pictures from the Internet

This tip was initiated by my sister who wanted to know how to download a picture from Facebook. This tip will work on virtually any picture you find on the internet. There are some protected pictures that the web developers have prevented you from downloading but this is a very small group.

To copy pictures from the internet:

- When you see a picture that you would like to save to use in a program or document or just to have saved on your computer, click on the picture to bring it into its own window. This will get you to the best quality image available. You might have to click a few times or you might get lucky and one click will do it. You'll know when you're at the best picture when your mouse no longer turns into a hand when it is positioned on the picture.

- Once the picture is in its own window, click with your right mouse button (Ctrl click for Apple users) and choose Save image as or Save picture as. The choice will be dependent on what internet browser you are using.

- The Save as dialog will appear allowing you to save the file wherever you would like.

- Choose a saving location and make sure the file has a name you will remember.

Now you can save all of your friends Facebook pictures and more. I showed this to a friend and she never sends an email without including a picture...not sure if that's good or bad.

Watch out for copyright issues if you plan on using the downloaded pictures for commercial use.

Tip #36 - Filling in Forms on the Internet

So there you are again filling in the form for your baseball/airplane/opera tickets and you have to give them your name, address, etc. What you need to do is click in the first field and, after filling in that field, use the Tab key to move to the next field. No need to move your mouse and click, just Tab from field to field.

Oops, missed a field and need to back up? Use the Shift key along with the Tab key to go backwards through the form. That's why the Tab key has a forward and backward arrow. It shows you that you can use it to go forward and backward, they just forgot to tell you about adding the Shift key!

When you get to a field, like the state or country field, which generally has a pop up list, you can type the first letter of the state to choose it. This is easy if you live in Florida as I do because there is only one state that begins with an "f". If you live in Connecticut, you have to type the "c" three times to get through California and Colorado. If you're one of the eight "N" or "M" states you might consider just using your mouse. Striking the N or M key eight times doesn't sound like a time saver.

Remember to use the Tab key rather than clicking each box; it really is easier.

TIP #37 - INTERNET BROWSER PAGE NAVIGATION

Forward and back buttons from different browsers

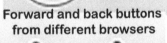

I believe that most people are aware that the Back button on the browser will get you to a previous page. This is a helpful feature of the browser allowing you to investigate pages knowing that you can always get back to a recent page by clicking the back button.

If you have strayed far away from your initial page you can get back there more effectively.

To return to previous web pages:

- Position your mouse on the back button and holding down the mouse button.

- This will display a menu showing you a list of your recent pages.

- Move your mouse down to the page you would like to return to and click.

This can save a lot of time if the pages between the one you're looking at and the one you want to go back to had many graphics that need to be redrawn. This will also help if you get stuck in one of those situations that the previous page bounces you back to the current page.

Here's an extra tip: if you're into keyboard shortcuts you can use Ctrl (Command) plus the left arrow key to move back to a previous page.

Tip #38 - Copying Text from the Internet

So you're getting ready for vacation and you have found lots of good information on a variety of web pages. The most common thing people do is to print out the entire web page, all eight pages, even though you only wanted the information on page three. A way around this is to select just the information you need, copy it and paste it into a word processing document.

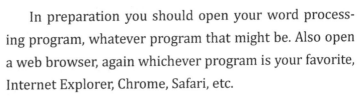

In preparation you should open your word processing program, whatever program that might be. Also open a web browser, again whichever program is your favorite, Internet Explorer, Chrome, Safari, etc.

Use a search engine to find a webpage that has interesting information for you to copy. This could be a recipe, directions, or travel recommendations.

After you have identified the information you would like to copy you need to select it. Do not use the select all command, because you will select too much information and it will be unmanageable.

Here's the steps to copy text from the internet:

- Select the text by dragging or by using the click – shift click method to select the text. You might remember from an earlier tip that when we want to select a range of text we click at the beginning of the text, scroll down to the end of the text area, hold down the Shift key and click at the end. You need to make sure the Shift key is held down before you click at the end of the text.

- Now that the text is selected you will copy it. Use the keyboard shortcut of Ctrl (Command)+ c or click with the right mouse button and choose copy. I know it doesn't look like anything has happened but remember that copy puts information on the Clipboard, a holding place in the computer's memory.

- Switch over to your word processing program. On windows machines use the task bar along the bottom of your screen, in the Apple environment click the program on the docking area along the bottom.

- Once your word processing program is on your screen, use the paste command of Ctrl (Command) + v. or click with the right mouse button and choose paste.

- Now switch back to your webpage and get some more text using the same technique.

You can copy and paste pictures too. In that case all you have to do is right click on the picture and choose copy, switch to your word processing program, right click and choose paste!

Tip #39 - Bookmarking a Browser Page

I spoke with two clients after posting the index for my blog. They both commented that they would bookmark the page if they knew how to do it! It's really easy to do but the directions depend on which browser you're using. Some browsers refer to Bookmarks as Favorites. Whatever it's called, it is the process that allows you to save web pages you've visited in your browser. These pages can be grouped together into folders or listed individually or added to a bookmark/favorites bar. The bookmark/favorites bar appears along the top of your browser window and should be used for webpages you use very frequently such as your email, calendar or Facebook page. All of the browsers listed here use Ctrl + d (Command on the Apple) to add bookmark or favorite entries.

Internet Explorer

The Internet Explorer is one of the browsers that uses the term Favorites to help you quickly return to web sites you've visited. To add to the favorites, go to a page you want to add to your favorites list and click the yellow star in the upper right side of your screen. A drop down menu will appear. Click on Add to favorites to add the current page to your favorites list or to the Favorites bar.

Mozilla Firefox

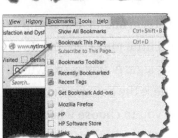

Mozilla Firefox uses the Bookmark menu to add bookmarks to its browser. Again you go to the page that you would like to bookmark and click on the bookmark menu. From the menu choose "Bookmark This Page". A further dialog box will appear so that you can choose whether this should appear on the bookmark menu or bookmark bar. From this dialog box you can also click on "Choose" to identify a specific folder for the bookmarks to be saved in or click New Folder to create a new folder group. Note in the screenshot to the left there are many folders that help organize saved bookmarks. This really helps if you are researching a topic and want to group your found pages.

Google Chrome

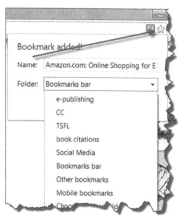

Like the Internet Explorer, Google Chrome uses a yellow star to bookmark a page. When you click the yellow star in the upper right side of the page, a dialog box appears for you to choose where the bookmark will be saved. You also have an opportunity to edit the name that will appear in the list as well as choose between the bookmark bar or folders. Although it is not documented when you hover over the star, Ctrl + d will bring up the bookmark dialog box.

AOL Browser

Many people log on to AOL through a desktop icon and then use the browser in the AOL program. AOL uses the term Favorites and they use a red heart to add to the favorites menu. When you click the heart a further dialog box appears allowing you to choose where the newly identified page will be stores. Note the Favorites menu at the top right of the screen. Clicking on the Favorites menu gives you access to all of your stored favorites.

Safari

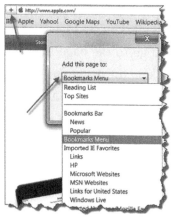

The Safari browser uses the term bookmark. To the left of the address bar you will see a little plus sign. To add the address in the bar, click the plus sign. A dialog box will appear allowing you to choose where the bookmark is saved. A further dialog box will allow you to choose whether the bookmark will appear in the menu or on the bookmark bar. To view saved bookmarks, use the book icon along the left side of the menu area.

FACEBOOK TIPS

Tip #40 - Like, Comment or Share on Facebook

If you're on Facebook you have probably noticed that under each post there are three possible responses, Like, Comment or Share. Today's tip will help you understand which is appropriate in which situation.

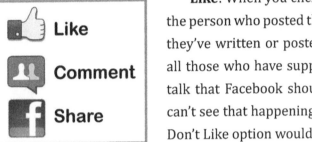

Like: When you click on the Like option you're telling the person who posted the message that you support what they've written or posted. The person sees the names of all those who have supported their post. There has been talk that Facebook should add a Don't Like option but I can't see that happening. Facebook is a happy place and a Don't Like option would set off negative vibes.

Comment: You Comment when you feel you have something to add to the post. Possibly you're supporting the position taken in the post or encouraging your friend. As with Like, the Comments are generally positive. During the political season the comments sometimes do get negative but that goes with the political territory.

Share: When you really like something and want your friends to benefit from or enjoy the post you would click on Share. The post immediately appears on your wall and all of your friends will be able to see it too. This is how things become viral on Facebook. Share is the ultimate compliment on Facebook. You are stating that the post is worthy of sharing with your friends.

If you notice that your own posts are not getting any of these responses you might consider whether or not you are posting too frequently. I always know when a particular friend is between college courses and has too much time on her hands. She posts dozens of cute animal pictures. I sometimes want to comment, "Enough with the cute animal pictures. Back away from the computer!"

Tip #41 - Managing Friends' Posts on Facebook

I'm sure you love your Facebook friends, well at least most of them, but there are some things my friends post that I'm just not that interested in, such as the high scores they get or their need for flowers, animals or buildings in the latest game craze. Have you ever considered unfriending someone just so you can be free of hourly updates? But you don't need to do that. There is an alternative.

Hiding friends posts

- When you see one of the posts you're not interested in viewing, move your mouse over the post itself.

- You will see a little down facing arrow on the upper right side of the post.

- Move your mouse on the arrow and click.

- From the menu click on hide... This particular post will be hidden and you will be given options about hiding future posts that are similar from this person or site or game feed. By choosing the game feed you will be able to view the posts from that person, but not the game feeds.

Whew! Did that cut down the number of posts you have to view? This is less aggressive than unfriending someone because of the items they post.

Just a word about making a selection from a menu, whenever you see a choice followed by an ellipsis (...) it means there will be further choices.

TIP #42 - FRIEND LISTS IN FACEBOOK

A list in Facebook is a way of controlling who has access to posts on your Facebook wall and whose posts you see. They are really easy to create and use. You already have, thanks to the Facebook people, three lists: close friends, acquaintances and restricted:

Close Friends: You can add your best friends to this list to see more of them in your news feed and get notified each time they post. You also have the option to turn these extra notifications off.

To turn off extra friend notifications:

- From your news feed, click Friends in the left column. You might have to click More to see the Friends section.

- Click Close Friends to view the list.

- Click the Notifications drop down in the top-right corner.

- Choose whether you want to turn off these extra notifications.

Acquaintances: This list is for friends with whom you don't need to stay in close touch. People on your acquaintances list will rarely show up in your news feed. You can also choose to exclude these people when you post something, by choosing Friends except Acquaintances in the audience selector pull-down menu when you create a post. By default it says "Friends".

Restricted: This list is for people you've added as a friend but you don't want to share with, like your boss or your in-laws. When you add someone to your Restricted list, they will only be able to see your Public content or posts in which you tag them. Public includes anyone on the internet --people who are not your friends on Facebook, as well as people who are not in your school or work networks, whether or not they have Facebook.

To see which list someone is on click the More link in the Friends section on the left of your screen and then click the See All Friends button at the top. All of your friends will be listed with an icon indicating which primary list they are on. You can also add them to additional lists here.

To create a new list:

- Click the **Home** link (along the top-right of every Facebook page)

- In the left column click the More link next to **Friends**

- Select the list you want to edit or click **Create a List**

- Name your list

- Search for your friends in the search bar at the top of the page, or add people from the **List Suggestions** on the right

Now when you post an update, choose the group who can see it from the list menu.

Tip #43 - Facebook Privacy Settings

The question I'm asked most about Facebook is, "who can view my information." The answer is, if you haven't changed the default settings on Facebook then everyone can see all of your information. They can't change the information but they can access your timeline and pictures and see who your friends are. If you are troubled by this, let me tell you where you can change these default settings.

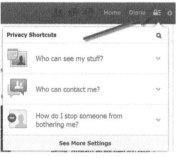

Because Facebook has been criticized in the past for making these settings hard to find, they have added a privacy icon that is available to you all the time in the upper right side of your Facebook screen. Click the privacy lock and you'll see Privacy Shortcuts such as: Who can see my stuff? Who can contact me? And How do I stop someone from bothering me? Click on the down arrow to adjust these settings. For more settings click the See More Settings at the bottom of the pull down list.

Setting most things to "Friends" will prevent anyone who isn't your friend from seeing the information. It is a good practice to review these settings periodically because the Facebook people are known to change the defaults sporadically.

GENERAL MICROSOFT OFFICE TIPS

Tip #44 - Extra Help for Microsoft Office

If you are a Microsoft Office user, you probably have needed some help to set tabs, create formulas, indent text, etc. Microsoft offers a new option in addition to the classic FAQ search.

On their website Microsoft has a page of Quick Start Guides for the 2013 version of its various programs in the office suite. These are in PDF format for easy downloading and printing. Each guide runs about five to nine pages depending on the program and covers the changes made to the software from the previous edition. Tips for using the program are included, as is compatibility advice for working with people who do not have Office 2013. Even if you are not using the 2013 version of the software I would recommend looking them over. The programs changed very little from the 2007 or 2010 versions. You can find these Guides by going to microsoft.com and searching for "quick start guides"

Free quick reference cards for PC and Apple for a wide variety of software and versions are also available from the folks at Custom Guide On-Line Learning. You have to fill in a form but I find that if you put in the comments box that you're just looking for a resource for personal use they don't bother you. Check out their guides at custom-guide.com and search for "quick reference".

Another place where people forget to look for help is YouTube. Yes, there are lots of crazy videos of dancers and talking animals there but if you, for example, want a training video on mail merge in any version of Microsoft Word, I guarantee you'll find dozens on YouTube. Some will be better than others, to be sure, but you probably will find one that will help you get through your project.

A fourth suggestion is to open any search page (Google, Bing, Ask, etc.) and in the search box enter your search term. If you were looking for webpages on mail merge I would enter, "word 2007 mail merge". I like to start my searches by entering the name of the program and version so the help is specific to what I'm seeing on my computer.

Remember, you're not alone even though there may be no one else in the room. The internet is just a click away.

TIP #45 - OFFICE - ACCESSING TEMPLATES

The hardest part of creating a document in any program is getting started. People often feel that they can edit a document just fine but they don't feel comfortable creating one. That's where the Templates in Microsoft Office can help.

When you click the File tab, New, you will see the different categories of templates that are available from the Microsoft website. These templates were created by users just like you and submitted to Microsoft for inclusion. Of course, the choices will be different if you are in Excel, where budgets and time sheets are included, than they are in PowerPoint, where there are templates demonstrating special effects or presentations designed for specific purposes such as selling or training.

If you don't have any templates available, check your internet connection. These templates are stored on Microsoft's website.

In the Apple version of Office go to the File menu and choose New from Template.

When you find a template you would like to use, double click on it. You might have to confirm that you want to download the template from the Microsoft website. The template opens on your screen and you can save the document just as you would any document.

So the next time you need to create a resume, design a flyer or create a budget, look to see if there is a template that could help you get started.

TIP #46 - PUSH PINNING DOCUMENTS

Here is a really important tip that will help you reopen frequently used documents and quickly revisit recently accessed folders.

Microsoft Office has always kept track of recently opened documents and you could see a list of the four most recent documents at the bottom of the File menu. In 2007 Microsoft expanded this list to display the last eighteen documents. At the same time they included the option to pin a document to the list so that it would never roll off, making it a cinch to open frequently used documents again.

When you visit the File tab in the 2010 and 2013 Office programs (or the Office Button in 2007), you'll notice that when you click on Recent on the left panel two columns appear to the right. The left column contains recently used documents; the right column displays recently visited folders.

Both of the columns have push pins available to the right of each entry. Click the push pin once to "pin" the document/folder to the menu. Of course, to unpin a document click the pin again.

This feature is particularly outstanding for those of you who are in a network environment where you have to do many clicks to navigate to network drives. Those drives are now available with one click.

Tip #47 - Drag and Drop in Word and Excel

Word's move arrow **Arrow in other MS programs**

On the Insert tab, the galleries include ite
your document. You can use these galleri
other document building blocks. When yc
with your current document look.

You can easily change the formatting of s
selected text from the Quick Styles galler
the other controls on the Home tab. Mos
theme or using a format that you specify

To change the overall look of your docum

Name	Last Name	House	Grade
l	Banes	Bella	
a	Fernandez	Bella	1
a	Sullivan	Bella	1

Many versions ago, Microsoft added a drag and drop feature to their products. Instead of cutting and pasting, you can now select, drag and drop. By dragging and dropping I mean holding the mouse button down to drag the information you have selected and releasing the mouse button to drop in another location.

The secret to dragging and dropping successfully is that you need to know where to position your mouse. In Word, after you have selected text, position your mouse on the selected text. You will notice that your mouse is now represented by an arrow rather than the traditional "I beam". The arrow shows you that you're ready to drag and drop. Hold down the mouse button and drag the text. As you do so you'll see a vertical line moving along with you. This vertical line represents the movement of the selected text to the insertion location. When you have the vertical line in place, release the mouse button. The text has moved to its new location. You'll find that if you're just switching words around or making small edits, the drag and drop technique is great. For moving text many paragraphs or pages away cut and paste is still your best tool.

In Excel you can drag and drop a single cell or a group of cells. After the cell or group of cells is selected, move your mouse to the border around the outside of the selected area. You will see the move arrow Microsoft uses in all programs other than Word. Hold down the mouse button and drag. Release the mouse button when you have reached your destination. If there currently is information in the cells being replaced, you will see a warning when you release the mouse button asking if you want to replace the contents. If the replaced cells are blank, no warning is displayed.

You'll want to try this drag and drop technique in other programs. In Powerpoint you can move whole bullet points around by dragging the bullet character.

I've used it successfully in many programs, including Gmail messages. Give it a try and look for the move arrow.

Happy dragging and dropping.

TIP #48 - GENERATING RANDOM TEXT

OK, I can hear you asking yourself, "Why would I want to generate random text?" Just bear with me. There are many occasions when I need to do this and it's very cool so I'm sharing it with you. Over the years people have said that they use it frequently too!

The programmers at Microsoft often need to generate random text to test software so they built in a "secret" macro that will produce a specific number of sentences

=rand(5,7) and paragraphs made up of real words, not computer Latin words. Try this out in your Microsoft Word program

Open a document in Word and type the text below then press the enter key (return in Apple world):

=rand(5,7)

Presto, the code you typed changed to five paragraphs each containing seven sentences. Keep in mind that the five and seven could be any two numbers depending on how much random text you need. So the next time you need to demonstrate something in Word to a colleague and you need some text to use, remember the code. It's pretty easy if you remember that rand stands for random.

If you would rather have Latin words, you can do that too. Type =lorem(5,7) in your document and then press the enter (return) key. The code is replaced with Latin text. Remember the five and seven can be any numbers you choose, the higher the number the more text that's inserted in your document.

TIP #49 - SELECTING TEXT

You're probably saying to yourself, what could be easier than selecting text. You hold down the mouse and drag across the text! Absolutely, but that's often the hard way and I'm here to help you become more efficient.

I watch people all the time change a word in an email or in a word processing document as they very carefully position their mouse at the beginning of a word, hold down the mouse button and verrrry carefully drag their mouse across the word. If they miss the first letter they have to start all over again. Other people work even harder by clicking at the end of the word and pressing the Backspace key, once for every letter. Ugh.

Here are some easy ways to select text:
- Selecting a word - double click on the word.
- Selecting a paragraph - triple click on the paragraph.
- Selecting a variable amount - click at the beginning of the text, hold down the Shift key and click at the end..
- Selecting the entire document - Ctrl (Command) + a (a for all).

Once you practice these selection techniques you'll use them all the time. Also, if you're replacing text you have selected, just start typing the new entry. You do not have to delete selected text first. Since it is selected it is ready to be changed or written over.

Tip #50 - Finding & Replacing Text

Finding

Using the search engine of your choice, you've finally found the entry you were looking for – the one with directions on how to plant daises. You click on it, but as you scroll down the page you see all kinds of information but none about daises. You scroll up and down and on the third pass, if you're lucky, you finally find what you're looking for. Whoa, let's stop the madness now.

You need to know about Ctrl + f (Command + f for my Apple friends), which is the universal keyboard shortcut for Find. You can execute a find in almost every document and on every webpage.

Once you do your keyboard shortcut to start the find, just type the search term. You may not actually see a place to type but strike those keyboard letters anyway. The first occurrence in the document or on the webpage will be highlighted. Tapping the Enter key will move you through the document identifying more occurrences of the term.

Replacing

A variation on Finding text is Replacing text. It shares the dialog box and you access it directly by clicking the Replace option on the Home tab, Editing group or typing Ctrl + h.

Most people will think about using the replace tool on their last proposal to change all of the occurrences of "ABC Moving" with "Acme Moving & Storage". While that is a helpful use of Replace, I use it to clean up documents that I copy from the internet or that people send me. They are often filled with manual line breaks, extra spaces and unneeded paragraph marks.

To replace special characters:

- Click the Replace option on the Home tab, Editing group.

- In the dialog box click the More button on the left side and then click the Special menu to view the options.

- If I wanted to replace all of the manual line breaks with a space I would find "Manual Line Break" in the list and click on it. Word inserts the code for that (^l) in the Find What box.

- Now click in the Replace with box and tap the space-bar once. You won't see anything in the Replace with box but the space character has been inserted.

- Now click the Replace All button and all of the manual line breaks will be removed.

Once you use this a few times you don't have to click on the More button and Special, you can just type the code ^l (l for line break) and click on Replace All.

Another code that I use frequently is ^p for Paragraph Return. I often get documents from colleagues that I need to import into newsletters or brochures. The colleague has typed the document using two returns after each paragraph. This has to be stripped out for my purposes. In the Find what box I will type ^p^p and in the Replace with box I will type one ^p. This is telling the program to find every occurrence of the Return/Enter key being struck twice and change it to one return.

Another example of this is when people get carried away using the Tab key. They will create lists by typing something like the first name at the left margin and then press the Tab key two or three times and type the last name there. They will again tab two or three more times before typing the phone number or other piece of information. These extra tabs need to be removed before this information can be put in a table or used in another format. In the Find what box I will type the Tab code of ^t^t and in the Replace with box I again use ^t. In this case I don't want to remove all of the tabs, just those areas of the document where there are multiple tabs together. After I click on the Replace all option I will often click on Replace all again. I am reading the search report looking for zero replacements made. Then I know that the document is free of these offending double (triple?) tabs.

108

TIP #51 - FORMAT PAINTER

Many programs have included a Format Painter in both the PC and Apple environment. The Format Painter allows you to copy the format from one place in your document and "paint" the format somewhere else in your document. By "format" we're talking about font, size, color, spacing before and after, text indents and the like. Using the Format Painter saves you time and duplicated effort when you want to format your document consistently. Instead of having to manually apply the font, font effects, paragraph alignment, and other formatting to each new area in your document, you can quickly copy all of the formatting attributes by using one button.

To use the Format Painter you need to start by selecting the **correctly** formatted text. How much you need to select depends on whether the formatting is a character format or a paragraph format. Character formats include font, color, size and style (bold, italic, etc.). Paragraph formatting refers to alignment, indentation, bullets, line spacing, borders, etc.

To use the Format Painter:

- To copy character attributes (such as font and font effects), double click the text. Use a triple click on the paragraph to select it for paragraph attributes (line spacing, indents, bullets, etc.).

- On the Home tab, Clipboard group, click Format Painter – once for one use, double click for unlimited uses.

- Select the text you want to apply the formatting to. Don't forget you can triple click to select a paragraph, double click to select a word. The text takes on the attributes of the new formatting.

- When you're finished, press ESC or click the Format Painter option once.

Be sure to look for the Format Painter in your favorite programs. It save lots of time and makes the formatting in your document consistent.

TIP #52 - MICROSOFT OFFICE'S HIDDEN DIALOG BOXES

When Office 2007 was introduced I thought the user interface was a great improvement over the classic menu driven access to commands. I also saw it as a huge training opportunity because everyone was confused about where their favorite commands had gone. Here it is many years

later and people are still looking for their favorite options. Many of these options never made it to the ribbons. You can look as hard as you want, but your favorite option may be in one of the hidden dialog boxes.

Microsoft put these dialog box launchers in the lower right corner of the appropriate group. If you look at the Home tab, Font group you will see one of these little boxes in the lower right side of the group. Clicking the launcher box will bring up the Font Dialog Box. Of course, you'll see many of the choices from the ribbon but Small caps, for instance, isn't included on the ribbon. Click on the Advanced tab in the Font dialog box and you'll see the Scaling and Spacing options.

Look around at the ribbons in all of the Microsoft Office programs and you'll see that many of the groups have a dialog box launcher. Click it once to see additional options.

TIP #53 - OFFICE'S VANISHING TOOLS

The new ribbon user interface on Office 2007 and 2010 is quite fancy, and once you get used to it, it's a lot of fun to use. One of its few downsides is that it's tall – far taller than a traditional tool bar. If you've got a 25 inch monitor that's fine but if you're working on a laptop or are otherwise pressed for screen space, it can sometimes be handy to collapse the ribbon and make it as compact as a regular menu.

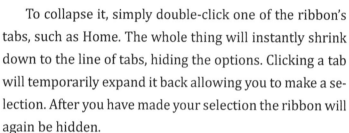

To collapse it, simply double-click one of the ribbon's tabs, such as Home. The whole thing will instantly shrink down to the line of tabs, hiding the options. Clicking a tab will temporarily expand it back allowing you to make a selection. After you have made your selection the ribbon will again be hidden.

A double click on any one of the tabs again will expand the ribbon to its original size. Now if you're tight on monitor space you know how to gain a few inches

Tip #54 - Roll Through the Office Ribbons

Because the Ribbons of options first introduced in Office 2007 were continued in Office 2010, it's safe to say that Microsoft will probably keep them around. As you probably know, clicking once on one of the tabs changes the ribbon you are viewing. While this is not difficult you might be interested in trying another way to roll through the ribbons

With your mouse on the ribbon area of the screen - that part is really important -- roll the wheel on the mouse. Rolling the mouse toward you moves you through the ribbons from left to right, rolling the wheel away from you activates the ribbons from right to left. This is a particularly helpful tip if you don't quite know which tab an option is on and you don't want to click the tabs individually.

If your mouse is not on the ribbon area the scrolling wheel will just scroll up and down your document.

Tip #55 - PowerPoint Show

The next time you create a PowerPoint presentation (.pptx) consider saving it one last time as a PowerPoint Show (.ppsx). The advantage of a PowerPoint Show document is that when you double click on the file, it opens immediately into the show view and you will not have to manually turn on the slide show.

On the face of it that may not seem like much of an advantage but here's the important thing to consider: anyone double clicking on the file would be put directly in the slide show view. So if you were to attach your PowerPoint Show to an email, the file would open and run when the recipient double clicks on it...even if they didn't have PowerPoint on their computer. A mini viewer is bundled into the file to allow the show to be displayed.

To get the greatest impact from this you should add timings to your presentation so it runs automatically or you need to let the viewer know that they have to click to move from slide to slide. You can accomplish this by adding back/forward arrows or just adding a note on the first slide telling the viewer to click to advance through the presentation. Any animations or transitions you added to the show would still be active. You can get really fancy and add a voice over to the presentation.

PowerPoint Shows are particularly popular around the holidays, ones showing snowy scenes indicating when you need to click to view the lights going on in the house or to click on the reindeer's nose to see it light up, etc. If you look at these files carefully you'll probably see that they are ppsx files.

TIP #56 - NAVIGATING IN A DOCUMENT

Here are a few really easy keyboard shortcuts to help you navigate to the top or bottom of a document. These also work if you are viewing a webpage and have scrolled down and want to get to the top of the page quickly or even if you're in your email program.

Ctrl + Home key (Command + Home for Apple) will get you to the top of the document.

Ctrl (Command) + End will get you to the end of your document.

You can also use the Home and End keys by themselves to get to the beginning or end of a line of text. I like to use the End key after I have edited the text in my email or word processing document to get to the right end of the line so I can continue writing my message.

The Home and End keys may be hard to find but I know you have them! Look on the right side of your keyboard. If you have a full sized keyboard the Home and End keys should be in the section between the alpha keyboard and the numeric keypad. If you have a laptop or a smaller keyboard you'll probably see them along the top right side.

TIP #57 - FREE MICROSOFT OFFICE ALTERNATIVES

Many of you do not need all of the power that's packed into Microsoft Office's suite of software and don't want to pay Microsoft's fees. If you fall into this category then you should consider downloading and using one of the free suites of software that can do many of the same tasks as Microsoft Office.

Two alternatives are: Apache OpenOffice from www. openoffice.org or LibreOffice from www.libreoffice.org. Both programs are offshoots from the original OpenOffice program. Apache OpenOffice is supported by IBM developers and LibreOffice is supported by freelance volunteers. Both are similar to Microsoft Office but they are FREE!

Both programs contain a word processor, a spreadsheet, a presentation application, a drawing application, a formula editor, and a database management application. You can seamlessly open, save, share and edit Microsoft Office files. The latest version of Apache OpenOffice was released in May 2012 and over 30 million copies were downloaded by the end of 2012. LibreOffice also has seen considerable success having been downloaded over 7.5 million times between January 2011 and October 2011.

So if you are one of those people who want to get away from what seems like Microsoft's monopoly on office-type software, consider downloading and using Apache OpenOffice or LibreOffice. You might also consider using a cloud based service such as Google Docs which are covered in tip # 98.

GENERAL EMAIL TIPS

Tip #58 - Addressing an Email

When you address an email you have three choices as to where the email addresses are inserted:

- The To line.

- The Cc line

- The Bcc line.

Each has a specific use. Let's look at them.

Putting someone's name in the **To** field indicates that the message directly affects that person or that something is expected from that person. You can send a message to as many people as your email service allows. If the To field contains five or fewer people it's nice to start the email addressing them individually. "Hi Pete, Sarah, Susan and Harold," for example. When you address an email to more than five people this becomes cumbersome so a simple "Hi Team" or "Hi All" will suffice. If your name appears in the To field in an email you receive, a response is generally expected.

The **Cc** field has been around for many years and was used in office correspondence to indicate a carbon copy. Since there is no carbon paper on the internet Cc has become known as courtesy copy. Including someone on the Cc line indicates that you are making them aware of the conversation but not necessarily including them in it. In general, if you are in the Cc field no reply is necessary.

And then we have the **Bcc** field. Bcc stands for blind courtesy copy. This field is used in two ways. It can be used to include additional people when you don't want the other recipients to know that others were copied. I'm sure you can think of situations where this would be helpful. Bcc is also used when you are sending an email to a distribution list and you don't want people to see everyone else's email addresses. In this case you should put all of the names in the Bcc field. This helps protect everyone's privacy. It's interesting to note that you can send an email with only names in the Bcc field. In the early days of email it was required that someone's name appear in the To box, that's no longer true.

To review:

To	**People are expected to take action.**
Cc	**People are being kept informed of the content, but no action is required from them.**
Bcc	**People are receiving the message without any of the other recipients knowing.**

Please share this tip with all of your friends but be sure to use the Bcc field for their email addresses.

Tip #59 - Reply vs. Reply All in Email

This is a hot topic for many people and it is an action that has gotten people in trouble over the years. There is a story about how in 2009, the State Department servers were crippled when email messages went out to thousands of diplomats and many of the recipients clicked Reply All to ask to be removed from the distribution list. This resulted in many other people using Reply All to tell folks to not use Reply All if they only wanted to send the message to the person that initiated it. All of this email traffic stressed the capacity of the system, forcing the undersecretary of state to send a cable (who knew people still used cables) to tell people to avoid using Reply All.

With our mailboxes filling up rapidly every day, let's do a little thinking before choosing between Reply and Reply All.

When you want to reply to an email you have two choices, Reply and Reply All. Reply sends the response to just the sender, while Reply All sends that same response to everyone who received the original email. Before you click the Reply button or Reply All button, ask yourself if it is important that everyone who has gotten the original message needs to know how you respond.

If you are part of a committee and a member is asking everyone's opinion about a topic, Reply All might be a good choice. If your friend has shared cute pictures of her puppy with a group of people and you want to respond, Reply would be the appropriate choice.

AOL is looking into displaying pictures of all of the recipients of an email rather than just the string of names to see if this helps remedy the Reply All problem. The thinking is that if you could see the faces of the people who would be reading the response you might think twice about the wisdom of using Reply All. I don't know where AOL thinks they would get all of those pictures but it might be an idea worth trying.

MICROSOFT OUTLOOK

Tip #60 - Signatures in Outlook - More than just your name

Most people who use Outlook at work are required by their employers to use a signature in their emails. This is a very important addition to your email because it becomes your business card. If you're not using Outlook, look for a signature feature in your email program. It's probably there.

Your signature should include your full name, title, company name, company tag line, mailing address, phone number, website and email address. Clearly, it would be tedious to type this on every email, which is where the signature feature comes in.

To create a signature in Outlook:

- Click the New Email button.

- In the Include group on the ribbon click the Signature option.

- Click on Signatures.

- Click the New button

- Name your signature and use the box at the bottom to fill in the information. Use the formatting options to add color and other text formats.

- Click Save

- Before you leave the dialog box choose one of your signatures to be the default for new messages and for replies. Click OK.

Outlook allows you to have multiple signatures. I advise my clients that they should have a second abbreviated signature for replies. This could simply be your name, phone number and email address. You'll see in the signature box that you have an opportunity to select one signature for new emails and another for replies.

In addition to using the signature feature to add contact information to new and reply emails, there are some other signatures you might consider creating. For example, if you have to send out a weekly reminder to the staff, you could create a signature with the contents of the reminder. Then, to start a new reminder email, click the signatures button and choose the appropriate "signature". Don't worry about selecting the current signature, since you can only use one signature in an email, the default signature will be replaced.

How many signatures do you think you need?

TIP #61 - SCHEDULING EMAIL DELIVERY

It should not surprise anyone that when you create an email and click the Send button (or Ctrl + Enter) the message is sent. But did you know that you can schedule an email message to be sent at a specific date and time in the future. I always thought this would make a good alibi if you were writing a mystery novel. "No detectives, I couldn't have done what you're accusing me of, I was here sending emails all evening!"

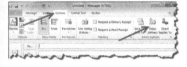

When you create a new email one of the options available from the Options tab is to delay delivery. When you click the option you will see the options dialog box where you can choose the date and time to deliver the message. It's important to note that your Outlook program **must be open** in order for the message to be released from your Outbox.

While you're in this dialog box notice some of the other delivery options. They include having replies sent to another individual. This is helpful if you plan on being out of the office and want someone else to receive replies to a specific email.

Also note that in this dialog box you can choose email receipts, both a delivery and a read receipt. A delivery receipt is generally not necessary because email gets delivered immediately. A read receipt can be helpful but the recipient generally has the option of having the receipt sent or not.

TIP #62 - ADDING CONTACTS FROM AN EMAIL

I find it amusing when I go to an office or home and see little pieces of paper around with email addresses written on them. When I inquire about them I'm told that the individual was making a note of the email address so that they could type it in their address book. Hummm, I see another training moment!

Microsoft, and other email programs, makes it really easy for you to add email addresses as long as you have an email from that person.

To add a contact from a received email:

- Find an email from the individual you would like to add to your address book and double click to open it in its own window.

- Move your mouse on to their address in the email and click with the right mouse button.

- From the menu choose "Add to Outlook Contacts".

- The new contacts window will appear with email address already populated. Often the person's name is also there but if not, type it in. Add any further information and click the Save and Close option.

That's it. That person has been added to your contacts! No more little pieces of paper with email addresses scribbled on them.

Tip #63 - Rules to Manage Messages

One of the most difficult tasks that people have is how to handle the large volume of mail they receive each day. There is a feature in Outlook that can help with this on-slaught: Rules. You can set rules for all of the emails from a person or group to automatically be moved to a specific folder, or a rule that plays a special sound when an email comes in from a person you designate or you can have a rule that forwards an email and then deletes it. Once you get the hang of them, you'll have all kind of rules.

The easiest way to create a rule is to find a message in your mailbox that is an example of the rule and would be affected by the rule. An example of this could be an email from your boss or from a listserve or, in the example shown here, from Smart Brief on Social Media, a newsletter I subscribe to. I want to create a rule that whenever an email comes in from this organization it goes directly to my "Social Media" folder where I keep emails about social media. When I have time I'll look through this folder but I don't want them cluttering up my inbox.

To add a rule to Outlook:

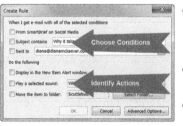

- Move your mouse on the email in the list and click with the right mouse button.

- Choose Rules, Create Rule...

- Select the conditions and identify the appropriate action and click OK.

- A window will appear asking if you would like to run the rule on the emails currently in your inbox. Running the rule is generally a good idea because it will test the rule.

That's it. The next time an email comes in to my inbox from Smart Brief on Social Media it will go straight to the "Social Media" folder.

You can use a rule to delete mail from companies that won't take you off their mailing list. Just create a rule that their mail goes straight to the deleted items folder or better yet, set it so the email is permanently deleted.

Tip #64 - Address AutoComplete

Outlook, along with many other email programs, re-members every address you have typed in a To:, Cc: or Bcc: field. This is good. When you start keying in a name or address, the program automatically suggests the con-tact in its entirety.

Unfortunately, you may have typed the address incor-rectly at one point or a contact has changed their email address and the program remembers the mis-typed and old as well as the correct information and suggests them indiscriminately. Fortunately, getting rid of entries you no longer want to appear in the auto-complete list is easy.

To Delete an Address from the Outlook Auto-Complete List

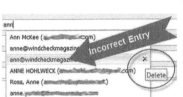

- Create a new email message in Outlook.
- Start typing the name or address you want to remove.
- Use your mouse or the down arrow key to highlight the entry you want to remove from the list.
- Press the Del key or click the delete X.

I really like the auto-complete feature and find it help-ful most of the time but, if for some reason you are not happy with it, this feature can be turned off permanently.

To prevent Outlook Address Auto-Complete entirely

- Select Tools/Options... from the menu.
- Go to the Preferences tab.
- Click E-mail Options....
- Now click Advanced E-mail Options....
- Make sure that "Suggest names while completing To, Cc, and Bcc" fields is not checked.
- Click OK.
- Click OK again.
- Click OK once more.

This feature is available in most email programs and you can give this solution a try. I also have noticed that in some programs you can right click on an incorrect entry and choose delete.

MICROSOFT EXCEL TIPS

Tip #65 - AutoFit Column Width and Height

When you begin an Excel spreadsheet, all of the columns and rows start out the same default width and height. The default column width is 8.11 characters or 80 pixels. The default row height is 14.4 characters or 24 pixels. As long as the information you put in the columns and rows fits in those constraints you are golden. Unfortunately the world isn't that organized and you will probably need to change the column and row sizes. That's where Autofit comes in.

I recommend you input a row or two of information before you adjust the column width. This will give Excel some idea about the type of information you plan on entering in the columns and rows and enable you to use the AutoFit feature. The rows and columns will be resized to the widest/tallest entry in the column/row.

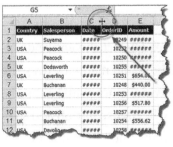

You can AutoFit one column or all of the columns depending on how many you select in the worksheet.

To AutoFit one column:

- Place your mouse on the vertical line that separates that column in the column heading from the column to the right.

- Double click the mouse.

In the screen shot, column C would be adjusted. If your mouse doesn't turn into a vertical line with a left and right arrow, you're not in the correct location.

To AutoFit multiple columns:

- If you need to AutoFit a group of columns, click on the first column heading and drag across to select adjacent column headings.

- Double click on the vertical line between any of the selected columns.

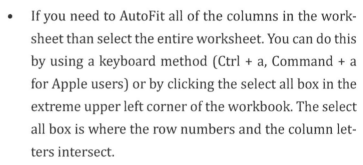

- If you need to AutoFit all of the columns in the worksheet than select the entire worksheet. You can do this by using a keyboard method (Ctrl + a, Command + a for Apple users) or by clicking the select all box in the extreme upper left corner of the workbook. The select all box is where the row numbers and the column letters intersect.

- Once the worksheet is selected, move your mouse on the vertical line in the column header between any two columns and double click the mouse button.

- Use the same strategies to resize the row height.

I have noticed that sometimes Excel resists the AutoFit double click. In those cases I select the entire document (Ctrl + a or the Select All box) and manually drag the column width to make it very wide, much wider than the maximum size I need. I release the mouse button and then go back between any two columns and perform a double click. Magically Excel now knows that you mean business and reduces the columns to a best fit option. You might also have to double click the horizontal line between any of the rows to reduce the height of all of the rows.

Tip #66 - Sorting Records

People love to use Excel to make lists. Lists of names, products, sales, you name it, someone has kept a list of it in Excel. The row/column structure in Excel makes it an excellent choice for these lists.

When setting up a list it is important that you do not leave any blank rows or columns within your list. In other words, don't skip a few rows because you want to break the information apart by department or da Now the fun begins. Use the controls on the left to change color themes, font, and other options. Experiment with the shape control to force your word cloud into different shapes. You can even upload a shape to customize the word cloud. In my example I used a dinosaur picture for my word cloud. When you're finished, click the Save option to save and print your creation or the Gift button to create amazing gifts.nything else. Don't skip a column because the entry spans two columns, adjust the column width (see Tip #65) instead. These blank rows or columns will make it difficult for you to sort or filter the information in your lists. It's fine to have information missing within a row or column but entirely blank rows and columns are a big no-no.

Once you have checked to make sure there are no blank columns and rows you're almost ready to sort. Before you sort, you should take a minute to format the header row, usually row 1, by clicking the row heading (row number) and choosing a format from the Home tab. I like making the header row bold and centered. This step identifies for Excel that row 1 is different and should not be sorted into the information in that column. It's really annoying to see the row label "first name" in the "f" section of names. If that should happen to you, use the undo button (Ctrl + z), add more formatting and try again.

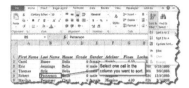

To sort your data:

- Click on a cell in the column you want to sort by. No need to highlight anything, just click one cell.

- Then click the Sort and Filter option on the Home tab in the Editing group.

- You can choose to sort ascending or descending. This will be represented by the A-Z button or Z-A button.

- Custom sort will bring up a dialog box so you can identify other types of sorts or a series of sorts.

You'll notice that when you do a second sort the first sort will be retained as much as possible. If you had a list of students with their grades and you wanted the names alphabetized by grade, you would first sort by last name and then by grade.

If you're going to do a lot of sorting you might consider customizing the Quick Access Tool bar to add the sort buttons. The Quick Access Tool bar is along the upper left side of your screen. By default it has Save, Undo and Redo. When you click the arrow on the right side of the QAT, you will see various tools that you can add. Click on a tool and it is now available for use. I always add Quick Print and New. Other choices depend on the program.

TIP #67 - FREEZING PANES

When working with an Excel list you often need to use many columns and rows, more than can fit in the height or width of the screen. As a result you have to scroll left and right as well as up and down to view your data. The problem with this is that important information is often in the first column or two and in the first row. When you scroll this information is no longer visible. That's where Freezing Panes is very useful.

For example, in the screen shot on the right, there is name information in the first two columns that you might want to freeze in place so that, as you scroll to the right, you can still see the names. You might also want to freeze the column headings in row 1 so you can see them when you scroll down the sheet.

To Freeze Panes:

- Click on a cell in your worksheet, remembering that when you Freeze Panes the cells above this cell and to the left of this cell will be frozen.

- From the View tab in the windows group choose Freeze Panes and then click on Freeze Panes again.

- As you will see, other choices are Freeze Top Row or Freeze First Column, which are useful if that is all you want to do.

Now take a test drive. Use the scroll bars to scroll up and down as well as left and right. Isn't it a miracle!

It always astonishes me to see how many experienced Excel users are struggling because they don't know the secret of freezing panes.

Here's a bonus tip for PC users. Did you know that the wheel on your mouse is also a button? It's particularly helpful in Excel where you need to scroll left and right. *Click* the mouse button. You'll see the circle pictured here. Now all you have to do is move your mouse away from this circle, to the left, right, above or below and the screen will scroll. The further you move from the circle, the faster you will scroll so be careful! This takes a little getting used to but it's easier than using the left/right scroll bar.

TIP #68 - LISTS

You may have been introduced to lists by the Excel program. When you start to create what appears to the program to be a list, a window pops up asking if you would like Excel to convert your data to a list.

An Excel list provides features designed to make it easier to manage and analyze groups of related data in a worksheet. When you designate a range as a list, you can manage and analyze the data in the list independently of data outside the list. For example, using only the data contained within the list, you can filter columns, add a row for totals, and even create a PivotTable report using only the data contained within the list.

You can have multiple lists on your worksheet, which allows you a great deal of flexibility for separating your data into distinct, manageable sets according to your needs.

NOTE: You cannot create a list in a shared workbook. You must remove the workbook from shared use first if you want to create a list.

If you already have entered information in an Excel worksheet but didn't use the list feature, you can convert the data area to a list.

To convert data to a list:

- Click any cell within the data area or select the data area.

- From the Insert tab choose List. If your first row contains column headings make sure you have checked the "My table has headers" box,

- Click OK. Now your data is in a table.

You'll notice that you have access to the Table Tools tab at the top of the screen, which will include an option to add a Total Row. If you add a Total Row, you'll see that each column has drop down choices for how you would like to calculate it.

So the next time Excel suggests adding a List to your worksheet, consider clicking on OK.

Tip #69 - Data Validation

In Excel, Data Validation refers to a feature of the program that allows you to limit the type of information that can be entered in a cell. You can limit it to a specific list of words, a range of numbers, only whole or decimal numbers, dates, time, etc. You even get to define the input message that appears when a mouse hovers over a cell with data validation, as well as the error alert message that would appear if someone were to enter incorrect information. Yes, you finally get to write the warning yourself!

This Excel feature is particularly important when you have multiple people entering data and you want to make sure the data is entered consistently and accurately. If someone has to order a minimum of 10 products and the data entry person enters an 8 in the cell, a warning dialog box appears. As part of the data validation you can customize the warning dialog box to clarify what the mistake is. In this case the dialog box might say "There is a minimum of 10 products. Please reenter the quantity."

If you want to limit the entries based on a list, you first type the list entries on a worksheet in the workbook, it doesn't have to be the same worksheet.

Creating a custom validation list:

- Select the column or cells that the Data Validation will apply to.

- Click on the Data tab and choose Data Validation (Data menu for Apple)

- From the Allow list choose List. You will need to identify the sheet and cells that the entries are coming from. You can do this by clicking in the source box,

clicking on the appropriate sheet and dragging to select the cells that have the data.

- You might want to edit the input message that the data
  entry person sees. To do this click the "Input Message"
  tab or the "Error Alert" tab and type in your message.
  The input message is displayed when the individual
  moves their mouse over the validated cells.

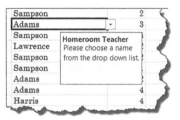

- When finished click OK.

You can imagine how useful data validation is to make
sure your data entry is consistent.

Tip #70 - Comparing Worksheets in an Excel Workbook

Even if you love Excel as much as I do, I bet at times you find it frustrating, particularly when you want to compare two or more worksheets in the same workbook. There's a lot of clicking back and forth between sheets trying to remember what one looked like while you looked at another. There is a better way.

What you're looking to do is create a new window of the active document to house the second worksheet.

Here's how to compare worksheets:

- From the View tab, Window group choose New Window. The new window is a duplicate of the original window. If you look carefully at the title bar, the new window is of course the same file name but the name is followed by :2.

- Then, still in the View tab, in the Window group choose Arrange All

- In the box that pops up, choose the way you would like your windows arranged. Click the checkbox "Windows of active workbook". Click OK. Clicking the checkbox for "Windows of active workbook" is particularly important if you have more than one workbook open.

- Click OK.

For my Apple friends or for those who are using a pre-2007 version of Microsoft Office, these controls are in the Window menu.

I generally choose arrange vertical which puts one window on the left and the other on the right. Tiled is a good choice if you have more than two windows open.

When you're finished comparing documents, just close the extra windows.

Tip #71 - Wrapping Text

There are some things people do in Excel that frustrate me to no end. I know that they either missed some fundamental Excel training along the way or that they've been using Excel for a long time and haven't noticed some of Excel's "newer" features.

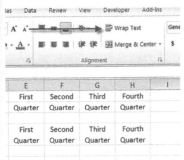

One format that I see people doing is breaking words apart on separate lines, as in the first group of headings in the image to the left. What you should do is type all of the words in one cell and then use the Wrap Text option. This will wrap the text on as many lines as are needed. If you resize the column the text will rewrap.

Note: If you want a particular word to start a new line you can use Alt + Enter to force a "line break" within the column.

Keeping the column heading in one cell rather than breaking it up across several rows is important for many reasons, including when you use advanced features of the program such as filtering, sorting, pivot tables and mail merge. If you were to create a pivot table you could be presented with multiple fields called "total" because that's the heading in the bottom row.

So save yourself lots of extra time and effort by using Text Wrap.

Tip #72 - Indenting Text

Another formatting mistake that is a big time waster is when people indent text before they start to type the entry by hitting the spacebar a few times. I don't know how they keep track of how many "spaces" they should add in each cell before typing. I have also seen worksheets where first level headings are in Column 1 and second levels are in Column 2 and so on. These columns are made very narrow. It looks pretty but it creates a mess when using advanced features in Excel.

The correct alternative is to use the Increase or Decrease Indent options.

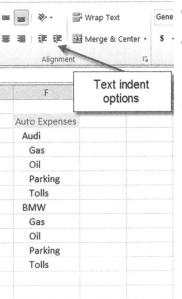

To create indented lists:

- Type the entries going down one row.

- Selected specific cells that need to be indented, remember you can use the Ctrl key to select non-consecutive cells.

- Click the Increase Indent option. Each time you click the Increase Indent option the text in the cell is indented a little further to the right. If you indent too far, you simply use the Decrease Indent option.

- Select more cells and indent those.

When I taught this tip to a group recently a woman came up to me after the presentation and told me I had just saved her hours of work every quarter. When she got reports that were exported from her financial program they needed to be formatted. She would double-click on individual cells and insert the appropriate number of spaces before each entry. She said everyone knew not to talk to her during the times she was doing this because it was such tedious work. Now she can accomplish this in just a few minutes!

If you apply both this and the previous text wrapping tip, you'll find that it takes a lot less effort to produce your Excel document.

Tip #73 - Creating Charts

Excel is an excellent program for creating charts. In the 2007 version, Microsoft did away with the Chart Helper and gave you the Insert tab from which you can choose the type of chart you want to insert in your document. Five steps later and you have a chart, right smack in the middle of your worksheet. You then needed to use the Move Chart command to get the chart on its own sheet. While this works, it's a lot of trouble.

Here's a simple way to create a beautiful chart:

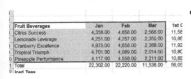

- Start by selecting the information you want to chart. Don't forget to select the row and column headings so that Excel will know what to call the value and category axis items.

- Now it's time to dust off the Function keys along the top of your keyboard. When they're nice and clean tap the F11 key. Excel will insert a new sheet in your document named "Chart1" with your beautiful chart displayed.

- The default chart type in Excel is a 2-D column chart with primary colors. If you would like a different kind of chart, use the options available from the Chart Tools tabs. (Formatting Palette in Apple).

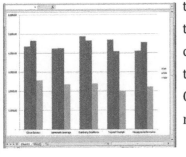

To make it easier for you to make your charts all look the same, you might consider creating a chart template or two. To do this, format a chart just the way you like your charts to look and then click on the Chart Tools → Design tab, Save As Template option. A dialog box will appear. Give the chart template a name. When you create your next chart you can click on the Change Chart Type option and click on Templates. Your templates will be visible. Choose the appropriate template.

Now that you have a chart of the first quarter, you might be interested in adding additional quarters when the information becomes available.

To insert additional data to your chart:

- From the data sheet select the information you would like to add. Don't forget to capture the column headings.

- Choose copy from the Clipboard group or use your keyboard shortcut of Ctrl + c.

- Switch to your chart sheet by clicking the sheet tab.

- Choose paste from the Clipboard group or use your keyboard shortcut of Ctrl + v

There is no need to select anything on the chart before you paste the information. Like magic the data is added to your original chart.

Note: If the information you want to chart is not in adjacent cells, you will have to use the Ctrl (Command) key to select it. In the image to the left we selected the salespersons names first, then held down the Ctrl (Command) key and selected the June data. Then we tapped the F11 key as described above.

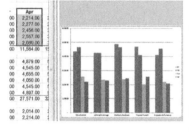

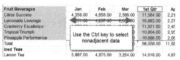

TIP #74 - WORKING IN THE GROUP EDIT

Wait till you hear this juicy Excel tip. Let's say you have created a workbook that has sheets for all twelve months and then you realize that you need to make the same change to all the sheets. If you're not aware of group edit you are relegated to making the change 12 times! Never again! What you need is group edit.

To go into the group edit:

- At the bottom left of your screen, click the first sheet you want to select (I'll call this the Jan sheet).

- Hold down the Shift key.

- Click the last sheet you want to select (I'll call this the Dec sheet). Now you're in the group edit mode.

The name of your document displayed in the title bar of the window will include (Group), as you can see in the image to the left. Make your changes to the active sheet (the sheet with the bold name) and the changes are made on all of the sheets. Quite a time saver, right?

Note: If the sheets you want to group are not consecutive use the Ctrl (Command) key to select them.

Here's an extra bonus of the group edit. If you are in the group edit and choose print, all of the sheets that are in the group will be printed. This saves you from having to switch to each sheet individually and printing it.

Eventually you need to exit the group edit, here's how that's done.

Once you've made your changes, you'll want to exit the group edit in order to make changes in individual sheets.

The method you use depends on whether or not you have selected all of the sheets in the workbook.

Exiting group edit:

- If all of the sheets in the workbook were selected, click on a sheet that is not the active sheet and you're out of group edit.
- If you have sheets in the workbook that were not included in the group edit, click on one of those and you're out of group edit.

TIP #75 - FORMULA AUDITING - TRACING DEPENDENTS AND PRECEDENTS

There are a couple of auditing tools available in Excel that are of great help when you are troubleshooting excel formulas, when you need to explain a spreadsheet to a co-worker or when you need to audit a spreadsheet for errors. The two primary tools are showing/hiding formulas and tracing dependents and precedents.

The Tracing tools are designed to identify graphically, using a series of arrows, the relationship of the active cell with other cells in your workbook. When you trace dependents, all of the cells that are dependent on the contents of the active cell are identified. Conversely, when you trace precedents, all of the cells that feed into or precede the active cell are identified with arrows. When you trace precedents the active cell must contain a formula.

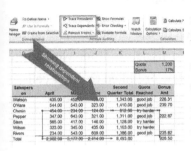

Tracing dependents:

- Open one of your worksheets that has formulas.

- Click on a cell that is used in a formula. This cell generally has a number rather than a formula in it.

- Click the Formula tab, Formula Auditing group, Trace Dependents (Apple and pre-2007 users - View menu, toolbars, Formula Auditing).

- You should see arrows pointing to the first level of dependency. Clicking on the Trace Dependents option again will show the second level of dependency.

- Continue clicking to show additional dependent levels.

If you print your worksheet while the dependency arrows visible, they will print also. If you wanted to print your worksheet at this point it would be helpful to print the row/column headings (the row numbers and the column letters) to help you identify the location of the cells. To do this click on the Page Layout tab, Sheet Options group, Print Headings (File menu, Page Setup, Sheet tab).

Use the Remove Arrows option to turn off the display of the relationship arrows. If you are an experienced Excel user I guarantee you'll use this tip a lot.

Tracing Precedents is exactly the same except that the active cell has to contain a formula, in other words, the contents have to be preceded by or linked to other cells.

TIP #76 - CONDITIONAL FORMATTING

I think those of you who work with Excel are really going to love this tip.

Conditional Formatting, as the name implies, allows you to automatically format a cell in a way that you designate, based on the contents of the cell. When the entry in a cell meets the criteria that you have defined, then the format of that cell changes automatically. The format can include a different font, font size, font style (bold, italic, etc.), font color and even border and fill colors.

Here's how to use Conditional Formatting:

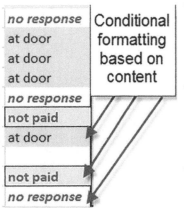

- First select the column that is going to have the special format by clicking on the letter at the top of the column.

- From the Home Tab, Styles group click on Conditional Formatting and chose New Rule... In Apple it's on the Format menu.

- Choose "Format only cells that contain" at the top of the box and in the lower part of the dialog box choose the appropriate condition.

- Now the fun begins, click the Format button. Use the Number, Font, Border and Fill options to make the entry as distinct as it needs to be.

- Click OK and then OK again.

- Repeat the steps for a second Conditional Formatting for the same cells or different cells.

Now when an entry in the cell changes, the format will automatically change. I have shown this to traders and financial people who jumped all over it. It can quickly highlight trading trends when the Excel worksheet is linked to live trading data.

Can you imagine using this for an accounts receivable worksheet? When the elapsed time from the date of the invoice reaches 60 days it becomes one color, when it reaches 90 days it displays another color format. The applications for this Excel feature are endless.

TIP #77 - DEFINING NAMES

Every cell in an Excel worksheet already has a name. The name of the cell is the column letter and row number, in that order, such as B27, G9. In addition to the default name, you can give a cell or a group of cells, a "nickname" that can be used in formulas, navigation and selection.

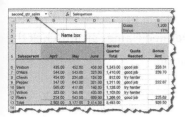

The name box is located in the upper left corner of the worksheet, above the row numbers. It displays the name of the active cell. When you hover above this box it shows the Name Box label. Clicking in this box will select the current name making it possible for you to type in a new name. After the new name is typed in the name box you MUST press the Enter key. Forgetting to press the Enter key will result in the name you've created being lost.

There are just a few rules when naming cells:

- A name must be more than one character and less than 255 characters. If you can't come up with a name that's shorter than 255 characters then you're not thinking hard enough.
- A name cannot begin with a number. It can, however, begin with a letter, an underscore (_) or a backslash (\).
- A name cannot contain spaces. If you want to name your cell First Quarter you can do so by taking out the space (FirstQuarter) or by inserting an underscore (First_Quarter).
- A name must be unique and must not resemble a number, cell address or reserve word. A reserve word is text used for functions and formulas. For example you cannot call a cell by the name SUM as it is already used in the function SUM.
- A name cannot use mathematical symbols such as + - * / <>.

If you examine the rules, you'll see that you really have a lot of flexibility in naming cells.

You may already have information in a worksheet and want to create names from this data. Here's how that works.

Naming cells based on selection:

- Select the cells of data as well as the row labels (see image to the left).

- From the Formula tab, Defined Names group, click the Create from Selection option.

- In the dialog box select the left checkbox.

- Click OK.

These defined names can now be used in formulas.

Tip #78 - Showing/Hiding Formulas

When you are viewing an Excel worksheet, you are seeing the result of formulas in the cells, not the formulas themselves. To view a formula you need to click on a cell and look on the formula bar above the worksheet where the formula is displayed. But what if you need to look at a lot of formulas or you don't know what cells the formulas are in, what's your option? The answer is simple. You can show all of the formulas with a simple keystroke.

To view your formulas on your active worksheet:

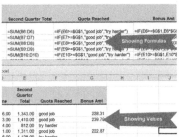

- Hold down the Ctrl/Command key and strike the tilde key (~) on your keyboard. The tilde key is below the Esc key, to the left of the 1 key and above the Tab key.

- If you're having trouble finding the tilde key this command is also available from the Formula tab, Formula Auditing group, Show Formulas option.

- Doing the same keyboard shortcut or clicking again on the Show Formulas option will toggle between showing and hiding the formulas.

The worksheet can be printed with the formulas showing. Be aware that, because formulas are often wider than the data in the cells, you often need to reset the column widths before printing and after printing.

TIP #79 - FILTERING RECORDS

When working with lists in Excel it's sometimes necessary to view a subset of the list. I have a list of members in an organization that I keep in alphabetical order. There are times that I would like to view only the people who joined in a particular year or who have been members 10 or more years. To hide all of the rows that don't meet my criteria I use the Filter feature in Excel.

You can access Filtering from the Home tab, Editing group or from the Data tab, Sort & Filter group. When you turn filtering on from either of these locations, you will see the program puts a pull down menu at the top of each column. When you click on these arrows you will see the menu has been populated with all of the unique values in the column. Using the check boxes you can select the values you would like to display and then click OK. Repeat this process in other columns until you are viewing only the records you need.

Keep in mind that using these filters, you are able to copy and paste only the visible records. I often use this technique when I want to email a specific group of people. After filtering the list and selecting and copying the email

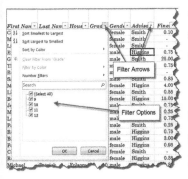

addresses I switch to my email program and paste the names in the To or the Bcc box of the new message.

Note that on the Filtering pull down menus, in addition to the unique data listed at the bottom, there are options for sorting the records. I often save my files with the Filters turned on because I use them so often.

Remember when you're setting up your lists, it is important that your lists do not have any blank columns or blank rows. It's OK if some of the cells don't have data but keep the rows and columns consecutive so that Excel recognizes contiguous data. If Excel does not identify the correct range of cells you will have to select the range yourself before you turn on the filter option.

TIP #80 - WORKSHEET PRINTING OPTIONS

Printing should be easy but for some reason folks have a lot of trouble with it. To help those folks, we're going to talk about the basics of printing a worksheet, including changing the orientation, adjusting the margins, printing gridlines, setting the print area and setting the percent of magnification for printing and printing multiple sheets at the same time.

When you are in an Excel worksheet and you choose the print option from the File tab, you are sending the entire sheet to the printer and printing it in a portrait orientation. If you would like to changes these options, clicking on the Page Layout tab and look at the choices in the Page Setup group.

The Page Setup group options:

- Margins option changes the margins for the document.

- Orientation option to change from Portrait to Landscape.

- Size option will allow you to change the paper size, the default is 8.5 x 11 inches.

- Print Area option allows you to print only a portion of the worksheet, you must select the area you want to print and then choose "Set Print Area" from the Print Area option. If you set an incorrect print area or need to change the print area, select a new area of the worksheet and choose Set Print Area again.

- Print Titles option will bring up a dialog box in which you can identify the columns and rows to repeat at the top and/or left of your worksheet. Just click in the Columns/Rows to repeat box and select the columns or

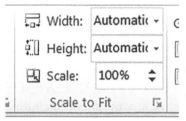

rows on your worksheet. The appropriate codes will be entered.

The Scale To Fit group options:

- The Scale To Fit group on the Page Layout tab is really important if you want the information to print on a specific number of pages vertically and horizontally. It's particularly important if the information doesn't quite fit on a page but almost does. You can choose "1" in both the Width and Height boxes and the page will be scaled down below 100%.

- Use the Scale box to increase the print magnification above 100%. If you want to print at less than 100% it's best to use the Width and Height boxes and let Excel determine the appropriate percentage.

The Sheet Options group:

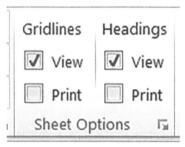

- This group is used to identify whether the Gridlines or Headings are visible and if they will print.

- The Gridlines are the light gray lines around the cells. Turning them on for printing helps when reading the worksheet printouts.

- The Headings refer to the column letters and row numbers. It is unusual for these to be turned off but is sometimes helpful for them to be printed.

One more tip. When you print, Excel prints the active worksheet. If you need to print more than one worksheet at the same time you'll need to select the worksheets. Remember to use the Ctrl key to select the sheet tabs for more than one worksheet. Then when you print all of the selected sheets will print.

There you have it. Hope this all helps when printing your worksheets.

TIP #81 - SCENARIO MANAGER

A helpful tool in Excel that allows you to store a variety of scenario models is the Scenario Manager. You create and save different groups of values and then switch to any of these stored scenarios to view different results.

For example, suppose are opening a sweet treats store and you wanted to find out your profit using different sales figures. You can use the Scenario Manager to create multiple scenarios on the same worksheet, and then switch between them. For each scenario, you specify the cells that change and the values to use for that scenario. When you switch between scenarios, the contents of the cells change to reflect the different values. It is helpful if you name the cells that you are going to be changing.

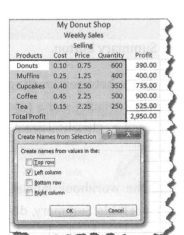

Entering information into the Scenario Creator is made easier if you have named the cells. If you're naming multiple cells you should consider using the Create Names from Selection option on the Formula tab, Define Names group. As you can see from the picture to the left, I selected the names in the left column all the cells that relate to that name.

To create scenarios:

- Open a worksheet and put in all of the information for one scenario.

- From the Data tab choose What If Analysis and Scenario Manager.

- Click the Add button.

- Name the scenario and identify the cells that will be changed in this scenario.

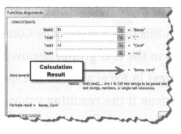

- Move to the Text3 box and click on the first name for the first person on the list.

- Check the formula result to make sure the formula is working correctly. If the formula is correct, click the OK button.

Notice that as you use the field boxes, you are given one more. You can concatenate as many fields as you need to.

You should now see in the first cell the results that you asked for.

To fill this formula down the column.
- Click on the cell with the formula.

- Position your mouse on the small fill handle in the lower right side of the active cell, the one with the formula.

- Double click the fill handle. Bam! The formula is copied in all of the cells in that column. It stops filling when it reaches a blank row.

You might need to adjust the width of the column so remember to double click the vertical line to the right of the column to make the column best fit.

If you have misspelled someone's name, make the change in the first or last name columns and the concatenated cell will change too of course since it's based on a formula.

Now you can throw the word concatenate into conversations and people will think you are a genius or a nerd.

Tip #83 - Finding Duplicates Records

I just had to compare two email lists. One was my Gmail contacts and the other was my Outlook contacts. I exported both of them to a file, deleted all but the name and the email fields, because that was all I needed, and copied and pasted them into one file, but then what? Many of the names were duplicates but how to weed them out? Then I remembered the Find Duplicates feature in Excel!

To delete duplicate records:

- This easy-to-use feature is on the Data tab, Data Tools Group.

- When you click the Find Duplicates option a window comes up asking in which columns you want to find duplicates. In my case I indicated only the email column but if you were trying to find all the duplicate records for people in the list with the same first AND last name, you would check those columns instead.

- Click the OK button. Poof, duplicates have disappeared.

- Excel will give you a report showing the number of duplicates found.

Remember, Excel **deletes** the duplicate records without confirming it so you might want to make a backup of the file before you delete the duplicates.

MICROSOFT WORD TIPS

TIP #84 - WORD'S COLORFUL UNDERLINES

I'm sure that you've noticed that your Word document is usually covered with colorful underlines. Starting with the 2007 version of Microsoft Office, the classic red and green underlines were joined by blue.

- The **red** underline indicates that a word is not in the program's dictionary. If you click with the right mouse button on the underlined word you will see a menu of choices beginning with spelling alternatives. If the word is spelled correctly you should choose "Add to Dictionary" so that it does not question your spelling of that word again. It will even offer your addition as an alternative if you misspell it in the future.

- The **green** underline indicates that there is a grammatical error. For example, if you type "The boys was happy." a green line will appear under "boys was" to let you know that the phrase should be either "boys were" or "boy was". The term grammar is taken in its broadest meaning. If you insert two spaces between words or an extra space before punctuation, you'll also see a green underline.

- The **blue** underline means a "possible word choice error." Even though the text is both grammatically correct and correctly spelled as is, Word thinks you might have intended a different word. The sentence, "The whether is frightful." will produce a blue underline under "whether" questioning if you wanted to use "weather". And in this case, Word is right.

You can modify how these are tracked in your document by going to the File tab → Options, which is along the bottom of the box. Click "Proofing" on the left. Use the

Check Boxes and the Settings button to customize the way Word proofs your document.

On the Apple you'll access these options by clicking on the Word icon in the upper left corner of the program window and choosing Preferences. In the window that appears, click on Spelling and Grammar.

Tip #85 - Creating Forms Using Tabs

Word is probably the most popular and appropriate choice for creating simple forms. The form we will be talking about in this tip is a form that will be printed and people will fill in by hand. We will discuss creating forms that folks can fill in electronically in the next tip.

The hardest part of creating a nice looking form is getting the line that people will be expected to write on correct. If you use the popular method in which you hold down the Shift key and use the underline key, you will create a line but the right side of that line will not stop at the same place for all of the form entries and just look messy. What you need to do is set a tab with a tab leader.

In order to do this we need to make sure the ruler is visible in Word.

To show the ruler:
- If you do not have a ruler visible along the top and left side of your screen, go to the View tab and in the Show/Hide group click the checkbox for Ruler.

- If you are working with an version of Word earlier than 2007 or are on an Apple you should go to the View menu and make sure Ruler is chosen.

Adding a tab to the ruler:
- Move your mouse up to the ruler, close to the right margin but still in the white area of the ruler. Your mouse should now look like an arrow.

- With the tip of the arrow just on the bottom edge of the ruler, click the mouse button once. You should see a small L shaped mark on the ruler.

Name_____

Address _____

Email _____

- Keep your mouse in the same location and double click on the tab you just placed on the ruler. The tab dialog box will appear. If it doesn't click cancel and try again.

- In the tab dialog box you will want to choose number 4 in the leader section for a solid line and then click on OK.

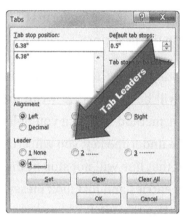

You have just set a tab on the ruler that has a solid line leading to it. In your document type "Name" and press the tab key once. You should see that a nice line appears from the end of the word Name to the tab you set on the ruler. Press the Enter/Return key and type "Address" and press the tab key. You can continue doing this down the page. Now that you know how to add tab leaders you should be able to add additional tabs on the ruler so that you can have "Cell phone" and "Home phone" on the same line with lines leading to them.

This tip might require a little practice. Don't get frustrated, you'll get it.

TIP #86 - CREATING FORMS USING A TABLE

Now that you saw in the previous tip the power of tabs and a tab leaders to create forms for printing, you're ready to learn how to create a form that people can fill in on their computer without upsetting the lines.

The tool we're going to use is the Table tool. The table tool inserts a grid of rows and columns in your document. By default, when you insert a table the cells have a border around them that will print if you leave it as it is. When we create our form we will remove these borders and just put in bottom borders where we would like information to be inserted.

Inserting a table:

- Click on the Insert tab, Table (Table menu, Insert table in Apple land).

- A grid will appear. Move to the second box from the left and click to insert a two-column, one-row table.

- The cells will be inserted in your document and the cursor will be in the first cell.

- Type the word "Name" and tap the Tab key twice. The first tap moves you to the second cell, the second tap gives you a new row.

- Now type the word "Address" and again tap the Tab key twice.

- In the left cell in line three of the table type "Email".

Now that we have all of our headings in place, this is a good time to adjust the column widths. Put your mouse on the vertical line that separates the left column from the right column. Hold down your mouse button and drag the line to the left. The left column will get narrower, the right column wider. Make the left column wide enough so that the entries in that column do not wrap. Remember, if you make a mistake you always have undo available (Ctrl + z)

Next we'll format our table so that there are only lines at the bottom of the cells in the right column. We first have to remove all of the lines.

Formatting the lines in the table:

- Select the entire table by moving your mouse on the table so that the table selection option appears on the upper left of the table. It is represented by a box with a plus sign in it. Click the table selection option once to select the entire table.

- From the Table Tools Design Tab, choose Borders, then No Borders (Table menu, borders on the Apple). Hang in, we're almost there.

- Select the cells in the right column only by dragging from the first cell down through the last cell.

- Go back to the Borders option and choose Bottom Border. Then back again and choose Inside Horizontal Border. Our borders are all set and the form is ready to be filled in.

OK, so this tip might benefit from a little practice but I think you'll see how great it is. Look around at other options from the Table Tools Design and Format options to split cells or merge cells.

TIP #87 - AUTOCORRECT TO AUTOMATE DATA ENTRY

I'm sure you've seen AutoCorrect in action in your Word documents. For those of you who like to press the Enter (Return) key at the end of each line (we'll talk to you at another time), you've probably noticed that Wo matically capitalizes the first character of the next line. Technically when you press the Enter key you've created a new paragraph and Microsoft thinks the first letter should be capitalized. You might not have noticed that Word will automatically correct other common spelling/keyboard errors without asking you about them. If you accidentally type "teh" it will be automatically changed to "the". Get the "i" and the "e" in the wrong positions in "receive" and it's fixed automatically. Imagine how many misspellings you would have if Word wasn't helping you!

I want to show you a terrific shortcut -- how you can create your own autocorrect entries so that when you type "usl" Word changes it to "US Lend Inc", the name of your company. When I was working on my PivotTable book I programmed autocorrect to change pt into PivotTable as I typed.

To create your AutoCorrect entry:

- Click the File tab→ Options→ Proofing→ AutoCorrect Options button (Tools menu, AutoCorrect for Apple users).

- Use the "Replace:" box to enter the text that you will type in the document (no spaces please).

- Use the "With:" box to identify the replacement text (see the figure to the right). When finished click the "Add" button.

- Now try it out in your document. Type your "Replace" text and press the spacebar or Enter key. Voila!

Now get creative. You can insert entire paragraphs of information. Maybe you need a disclaimer inserted in some documents, make an autocorrect entry for it. In that case you would either find a document that has the text or type it in a document and select the text. Then go to the File tab → Options → Proofing → AutoCorrect Options as we did earlier. The "With:" box is automatically populated with the selected text. Type an entry in the replace box, click Add and you're done.

Note: Be sure that your "Replace" text doesn't spell a word or you'll never be able to use that word again! I remember showing this to a group of Account Representative Executives. Our first thought was to use "are" as the Replace word...saner heads prevailed and we used something else.

Tip #88 - Automatic Bullets/Numbered Lists

More than ten years ago Microsoft introduced Auto-Correct to the world. We talked in a previous tip about how great this feature is. However, there is one aspect of this feature that really frustrates people...it's how Word automatically thinks you're starting a bulleted or numbered list as you type when you start a paragraph with an asterisk (*) or with a number.

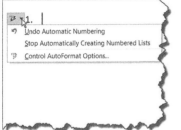

Microsoft is just trying to be helpful but I do agree this can be a little frustrating. However there's an easy solution. All you have to do is look for the little lightning bolt control menu that appears whenever the program automatically "corrects" something. Move your mouse on the menu and click on what you want the program to do. As you can see from the screen capture you can undo Automatic Numbering, Stop Automatically Creating Numbered Lists (forever) or Control AutoFormat Options... The last of these choices will bring up the AutoFormat Options dialog box where you can review other options that you might want to change.

AutoFormat is not just a Word feature. Those of you who use Excel, PowerPoint, Outlook, and other Microsoft programs will recognize it too. Just look for the lightning bolt to control automatic changes.

TIP #89 - COMPARING DOCUMENTS

There I was merrily working on a document for a client, making changes and saving frequently, as I should, when I noticed I was not working on the most current version of the document. Ugh. I now had two versions and needed to combine them into one file. Fortunately Word has our backs on this and we can use the Compare Documents feature. Whew.

To compare documents:

- Click the Review tab and, from the Compare group, choose Compare and then Compare again. The Compare Documents dialog box shows up.

- Select the original document from the Original Document drop-down list. If you can't find the original document, click the folder icon to browse for it.

- Select the edited document from the Revised Document drop-down list. As with the original document, you can locate the revised one by clicking the folder icon to browse.

- Click OK. Word compares the two documents and notes all changes. Then it displays a list of changes, the compared document with changes marked, plus the original and revised documents.

Now use the Accept/Reject options on the Review tab to go through the document identifying the changes you would like to keep or reject.

Whew, saved again by a feature in Microsoft Office.

194

Tip #90 - Important Word Processing Formatting Tips

I see a lot of frustration when people are creating documents that have bullets and numbered lists. One of the things that makes bullets and numbered lists so convenient is that when you press the Enter key, you automatically get a new bullet or number. Well that's all well and good but suppose you just want a new line, not a new bullet or number. Ah, you need to know this secret.

New line	Shift + Enter
New page	Ctrl + Enter

When you press the Enter key you are creating a new paragraph and the new paragraph carries the same formatting (bullets/numbering) as the previous paragraph. To get a new line you need to hold down the Shift key and tap the Enter key. This is particularly helpful when you want to create second lines below bullets and numbers. This new line is sometimes called a "soft return". I can see your blood pressure lowering already.

Another helpful keyboard shortcut in Word will give you a manual page break so that you don't have to press the Enter (Return) key X number of times until a new page miraculously materializes. When you want to insert a new page hold down the Ctrl key and tap the Enter key.

The beauty of this is if you add information above the page break you just inserted, the words on the next page will not bump down too. On the Apple you'll have to work a little harder to get a page break. A page break is Fn + Shift + Return. You hold down the Fn and Shift keys at the same time and then tap the Return key.

Tip #91 - Multilevel Lists

For those times when you need to make an outline or other kind of multilevel list, Word has a dandy feature to help you. On the Home tab ribbon you'll find the multilevel list option in the Paragraph group. Clicking on the down triangle reveals the assortment of lists that are available including numbered and bulleted lists. But that's not all. These basic list types can be customized.

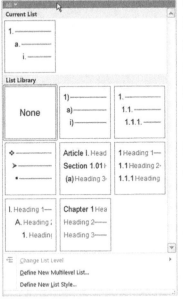

Inserting a multilevel list:

- Click in your document where you would like to insert the multi level list.

- From the Home tab, Paragraph group, click the Multilevel list option and choose the type of list you want to create.Clicking on one of the choices will insert the first level of the list.

- Type your entry and press the Enter/Return key to duplicate the level that you were just using. For example if you are using a multilevel list that has numbers, the first paragraph will have a "1" inserted at the beginning and pressing the Enter/Return key will insert the number "2".

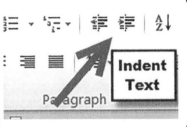

- To indent to the second level you need to press the Enter/Return key, which will repeat the previous level. While your curser is in this new paragraph, use the Increase Indent option to indent to the second level or the next level down from the previous paragraph.

- Use the Decrease Indent option to move the paragraph back to the left.

I sometimes find it easier to format the list after I've typed it. I turn on the multilevel list feature and then just type it as one long list. I then select all of the text that needs to be indented and click on the increase indent option. I find Word plays nicer using this approach.

TIP #92 - TRACK CHANGES

Track Changes is a valuable tool in Word that allows you to keep track of all of the revisions you make to a document so that you can easily identify them. This feature is most frequently used by people sharing documents. One person creates the document and sends it to another for editing. The second person turns on Tracking Changes, and makes the changes, saves them and returns the document to the first person. The originator of the document is able to clearly see the editing changes. In addition, the originator is able to go through the document revision by revision accepting or rejecting the changes.

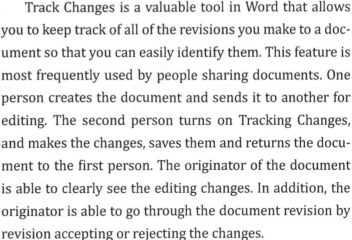

If more than one person needs to make changes than each person would have to make sure that Tracking Changes was on. Then their revisions would automatically be made in a different color, making it easy to see all of the revisions made by an individual. Moving your mouse on a revision will also show you the name of the individual and the date and time the revision was made.

To turn on Track Changes:

- On the Review tab, Tracking group click on Track Changes.

- Click on Balloons (to the right of Track Changes) to see the options for how to show the markup. My preference is to show the revisions in line as opposed to in balloons off to the side of the change.

That's it! Now as you make changes in your document you will see the words with markups to indicate deletions and insertions will be made in a different color.

An elderly client of mine, working on her third Master's degree would retype any documents that her instructors had reviewed with tracking because she didn't know how to accept the changes!

How to accept or reject edits:

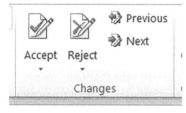

- On the Review tab, Changes group click on the Next option

- The first change will be selected.

- Use the Accept or Reject options to accept or reject the change.

- The change will be made and the next change will be selected automatically. Continue through your document accepting or rejecting the edits.

- You can also click the down arrow below the Accept or Reject options to accept or reject all of the revisions.

Once you're finished checking the document, don't forget to save it.

Tip #93 - Styles

Microsoft has been trying for years to get you to use their built-in styles in Word to make the formatting of your document easy and consistent -- and yet you continue to resist their efforts. In the 2007 and later versions of Microsoft Word they have taken these styles and splashed them across the Home ribbon, hoping to entice you with them.

At a very minimum you should notice that there are two primary styles, Normal and No Spacing. For those of you who do not like Microsoft's new spacing defaults of extra spacing added between paragraphs and within paragraphs, select your document (Ctrl/Command + a) and click on the No Spacing style and all of that extra space will be removed. Of course you'll have to go back to manually hitting the Enter/Return key twice between paragraphs.

Styles can make formatting long documents mindlessly easy. When you are starting a new area of your document all you have to do is click on one of the heading styles (Heading 1, Heading 2, Heading 3, etc.) in the Styles group of the Home tab. The formatting of the paragraph will change to conform to the choices Microsoft has made for that style. These formatting choices include font, color, size, alignment, spacing, pagination, etc.

If you like the idea of using styles but don't like the formats Microsoft has developed, you can right click on the style on the ribbon and choose Modify. Use the Formatting options in the window or click the Format button to access additional options. If you have already formatted your document with styles, all of the paragraphs that use the modified style will change automatically.

Another advantage to styles is that Word uses them as the basis for Table of Contents. If you use Headings 1, 2 and 3 styles in your document, Word will develop your TOC automatically. Once the TOC is developed you can update it by clicking in the TOC area and pressing the F9 key on your keyboard. A dialog box will ask if you want to update just the page numbers or the entire table.

Styles are a real time saver for long documents. Once you feel comfortable with them you'll wonder why it took you so long to use them. There are styles in Excel also so look for them there too.

Tip #94 - Document Map

In the last tip we talked about using Styles in a document to quickly and consistently format a document. Another reason for using styles is that they are the basis for Document Maps which aid in document navigation. They also are extremely helpful for rearranging the contents of documents.

My document for this book would have been tedious to navigate if I didn't use the Document Map. By applying Heading 1, 2 and 3 styles to my document, a hierarchal map was developed that I can display by clicking on the View tab, Show group, Navigation Pane. A pane appears on the left side of the screen that shows the first few words of the formatted paragraph. Clicking on a heading navigates to that part of the document.

Beginning with the 2010 version of Word, in addition to navigation, whole sections of the document can be moved around by dragging the headings up and down in the Document Map. No selecting, cutting and pasting, just drag the heading and release the mouse button. Because my title style included the numbering feature, my tips were automatically renumbered when I moved them in the document. This is important information for attorneys, engineers, architects and anyone else that uses numbered paragraphs.

Tip #95 - Is Your Document Written at the Right Level For Your Readers?

There are times when it's useful to know the grade reading level of material you are writing. I'll show you how to turn this feature on in Word and also give you some internet options if you don't have Word.

To turn on the radiability feature on in Word:

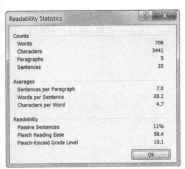

- Click on the File tab (in Office 2010) or the Office button (in Office 2007).

- Select Options.

- On the left side of the screen click on Proofing.

- Click the checkbox to "Show readability statistics".

- Click OK.

The next time you spell check your document (Review tab, Proofing group, Spelling & Grammar) the Readability Statistics dialog box will appear upon completion.

The Flesch Reading Ease result is an index number that rates the text on a 100-point scale. The higher the score, the easier it is to understand the document. Factors that influence the score are the average number of sentences per paragraph, the average number of words per sentence and the average number of characters per word. Authors are encouraged to aim for a score of approximately 60 to 70. The Flesch-Kincaid Grade Level is a rough measure of how many years of schooling it would take someone to understand the content.

Internet websites are available that will test the readability of your document. One of them is http://www.readability.info/. At this website you can not only paste a document in for analysis but you can also enter a URL (website address) and the radiability website will analyze the websites readability level. This is particularly helpful for web content providers.

FUN PROJECTS & PROGRAMS & OTHER STUFF

Tip #96 - Picasa Photo Organizer

Picasa is a free program from our friends at Google (www.picasa.google.com). It is a terrific program to help you organize, edit and share all of those pictures you have downloaded from your camera. It is easy to download the program and the download page has lots of directions to guide you through the process.

I'm so excited about Picasa because it allows you to see your pictures in a continuous display without having to double click on folder after folder to see what's inside them. Unlike many other programs, Picasa doesn't hold your pictures captive in the program but merely displays the pictures that already exist somewhere on your computer. When you use Picasa, the folder that the pictures are stored in is listed on the left side of the screen and thumbnails of the pictures are on the right side of the screen. When you single click a folder the thumbnails of the photos in that folder will appear at the top of the preview area. You can also use the scroll bar on the right side of the screen to scroll through your pictures.

Changing the date of a folder:

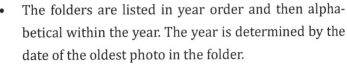

- The folders are listed in year order and then alphabetical within the year. The year is determined by the date of the oldest photo in the folder.

- Change the date by double clicking on the folder.

- In the dialog box click the down arrow to the right of the date.

- Use the calendar to choose a new date or click the "Today" option to add today's date to the folder.

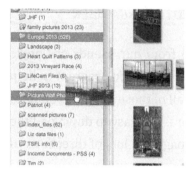

If you see any pictures that are misfiled, you can drag the pictures from the thumbnail area on the right to the appropriate folder listed on the left. When you release the mouse button a window will appear confirming your movement. If you see any pictures you would like to delete, click the picture and press the delete key on your keyboard.

One of the best features is the ability to edit pictures. When you double click on a picture you are in the editing screen. These tools include cropping, straightening and many color/lighting correcting features. Play with the editing tools until you are happy with the revised picture. Then choose Save from the File menu. You will see a box that alerts you to the fact that Picasa saved the unchanged original of the picture as well as the revised copy.

It is important that you save your changes because unsaved changes are displayed on the screen but will not be implemented if you upload this picture for use in sharing or project creating. The original of the picture is saved in a folder labeled "Picasa" that is created in the pictures folder. If you're not the trusting type you can always chose "Save a copy" from the File menu before you begin editing the picture. Then you're sure you've always got the original.

Apple users may point out that they have iPhoto and don't need Picasa. I believe Picasa is considerably better than iPhoto. Give it a try and see if you don't agree.

TIP #97 – COPYING PICTURES FROM YOUR CAMERA USING PICASA

Not only does Picasa make it easy for you to organize the pictures currently on your computer but it's also a great tool to help you download pictures from your camera. You may already be using a program that came with your camera or iPhoto, if you have an Apple, but I think you should consider using Picasa to accomplish this task. If you haven't downloaded Picasa yet, go to <u>www.picasa. com</u> and get your free copy.

When you open Picasa you can see the "Import" button in the upper left corner. If your camera is attached to your computer and your camera is turned on, you will see the pictures that are on it when you click the Import button. The pictures will be displayed in date groups with the oldest pictures at the top of the list.

Here's how to download in three easy steps.

- Select pictures to import into a folder. If you are selecting a consecutive group of pictures you can click on the first picture, hold down the Shift key and click on the last picture. If your pictures are not consecutive you'll have to use the Ctrl/Command key to select specific shots.

- At the bottom left of the window, name the folder

- Click the Import Selected button

A new folder will be created on your hard drive in your My Pictures folder with the name you gave it. Repeat until all of the pictures you want to copy have been downloaded.

There it is, downloading in three easy steps.

Tip #98 - Google docs

Google Docs is a versatile cloud-based service that features an array of office applications that compete with Microsoft Office. Since it is cloud-based there is nothing to download and you can access your files from any computer. All you need to access Google Docs is a Google account, which can be setup using any email address, Gmail is not required. Once you log on to your Google account, click the Apps button on the upper right side of the screen and then click Drive to access the Google docs area. Click the Create button to choose the type of document you would like to start. The document opens in a new tab in your browser.

Your choices for a new document include word processing (Document), spreadsheet (Spreadsheet) slide presentation (Presentation), form (Form) and even a drawing tool (Drawing).

The word processing program is quite powerful and has many of the frequently needed tools. It is certainly not as powerful as Microsoft Word but for most people, it has all of the features they need.

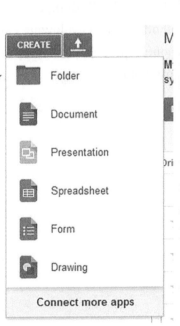

The presentation program allows you to enable real-time viewing of presentations, online, from separate remote locations. You can also add images, slides and videos and embed your presentations in a website, which will provide access to them to a wide audience.

The spreadsheet application features custom formatting for spreadsheets, charts and gadgets.

The form application offers a unique way to create questionnaires that can be filled in and submitted online. The results of the questionnaire are then placed in a spreadsheet. The results can then be plotted on charts for analysis.

The drawing tool enables you to quickly scribble a rough design for a new idea or build a flowchart using shapes and lines. You can insert these drawings into your documents, spreadsheets and presentations.

But, not only do you have a complete cloud-based office at your disposal, you can also upload your creations and share them with people online, using real time chat to communicate and collaborate back and forth. I recently invited a class to make changes to a document. The participants were able to see on the projected screen all of the changes that were being made simultaneously by everyone in the room!

As you can see, Google docs gives Microsoft a real run for the money, and Google docs is FREE. Google's programs also work on iPads and other tablets, allowing you to use them to create documents, spreadsheets and presentations and email and share them.

Tip #99 - Making Word Clouds

I think you'll enjoy this easy and fun project that will impress friends and family.

A word cloud is a collection of words displayed creatively. It was initially used to demonstrate visually the frequency of words on a web page and was a tool in optimizing it for search engines. Search engines rate a page by these word frequencies and store them in their databases and use them when you are doing a webpage search. The more frequently a word appears on a webpage, the larger the font size for that word in the world cloud. Now word clouds are used for many reasons, including creating unique gifts for special events. An internet search for "word clouds" will yield many websites. The results shown here were created by the website www.tagxedo.com.

You create a word cloud by typing a list of words in a word processing program – any program will do – and copying and pasting them into the tagxedo website or by typing them directly in on the website. The reason I suggest the word processing method is that I like to spend time thinking about the words I might use. Either method is fine. In the Fred Flintstone example shown here, I typed the words into a word document. My list included all of the main characters in the TV program as well as some associated terms. For names or multi word terms use the tilde key to create a non-breaking word, for example Fred~Flintstone. The tilde key is above the Tab key and to the left of the number 1 key. Don't forget to use the Shift key to access it.

To create a word cloud:

- Create your list of words in your word processing program.

- Select the text (Ctrl/Command + a) and copy it (Ctrl/Command + c).

- Open your browser and go to www.tagxedo.com.

- Click the Create button to open the creation window.

- Click the Load button and paste your list (Ctrl/Command + v) in the Enter Text box.

- Click the Submit button.

Now the fun begins. Use the controls on the left to change color themes, font, and other options. Experiment with the shape control to force your word cloud into different shapes. You can even upload a shape to customize the word cloud. In my example I used a dinosaur picture for my word cloud. When you're finished, click the Save option to save and print your creation or the Gift button to create amazing gifts.

I've created word clouds for friends and clients to celebrate milestones and I even used one in a business card design.

Have fun creating your own word clouds.

Tip #100 - Great FREE Fonts for Downloading

If you love experimenting with fonts as much as I do, you'll love Google's free font downloading service. Over 600 fonts are now available and the number is growing daily. You can download as many of them as you want. Just go to www.Google.com/fonts and start having fun.

Downloading the free Google fonts:

- Use the filter tools on the left of the screen to limit your selection by categories and styles.

- When you find a font you like, click the "Add to Collection" button to save your choices.

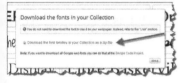

- When you're finished making your selections click the "Download Your Collection" link in the upper right side of the screen. You'll see a window telling you that you don't have to download to use the fonts on the internet but you'll need to download them for use on your computer. This will download a zip file with all of your fonts.

- Once the zip file is downloaded you need to open it and extract all of the font files. Unfortunately this does not install them.

- To install your fonts double click on each font and then click the Install button.

It sounds like a lot of work but it's well worth the effort.

When you're looking for fonts to download consider choosing fonts with multiple styles. Click the "Show all styles" link to preview the font family. Four styles will generally give you normal, bold, italic and bold italic. Fonts with greater style choices will print better than those with just one style. You can change the sample text that's displayed for the fonts. This is helpful if you want to use the font for a specific group of words. Some fonts are clearer for individual letters than others. I was once working on an invitation and the location was on the Courtney Campbell Causeway. The font I initially thought I would use had an upper case "C" that looked like a "P". Suddenly my invitation had people going to the Pourtney Pambell Pauseway! That would not do.

So now that you have lots more fonts to choose from, promise me you won't be using Comic Sans anymore.

Another internet resource for fonts — not all are free but it's still worth looking at them — is www.myfonts.com. They have an impressive library and even offer a free font identifier. If you love fonts as much as I do, you can sign up for their monthly newsletter which has many interesting articles.

APPENDICES

RECAP OF KEYBOARD SHORTCUTS

Undo	Ctrl + z
Cut	Ctrl + x
Copy	Ctrl + c
Paste	Ctrl + v
Print	Ctrl + p
New	Ctrl + n
Open	Ctrl + o
Save	Ctrl + s
Top of document	Ctrl + Home
End of document	Ctrl + End
Select All	Ctrl + a
View Desktop	Windows + d
Switch Programs	Alt + Tab (Command on Apple)
Find	Ctrl + f
Repeat Action	Ctrl + y
Lock desktop	Windows + l
Opens the Run Program Dialog	Windows Key + r
Minimize all windows	Windows Key + m
Maximize all windows	Windows Key + Shift + M
Find files on your computer	Windows Key + f
Open Windows Explorer/My Computer	Windows Key + e
Duplicate Objects	Ctrl + drag
Help	F1

Remember on the Apple use Command for the Ctrl key.

ALT CODE REFERENCE SHEET

Have you ever wondered how people inserted special characters such as smiley faces, hearts, arrows, etc. into their emails, Tweets, Facebook posts or worksheets? They probably used Alt codes to accomplish it.

Alt codes have been around for decades and were used by early programmers. I have compiled a list below for your use. If you want to print out a copy, note the page number that the reference sheet is on and go to the File menu and choose print. In the print dialog box click the "pages" option and type in the page number and then click print.

For Apple users I have included a special sheet of what you need to do to add accents and special characters to your documents. Keep scrolling down this document to view the sheet.

Alt Code Reference Sheet

Use in all text editing programs including Word, Facebook, Email and Excel

Hold down the Alt key then enter the code using the numeric keypad. Make sure Num Lock is on.

Bullets & Emoticons		Filled Arrows		Greek		Letters with Accents			
							Uppercase		Lowercase
Alt + 1	☺	Alt + 16	►	Alt + 224	α				
Alt + 2	☻	Alt + 17	◄	Alt + 225	ß	Alt + 0192	À	Alt + 0224	à
Alt + 3	♥	Alt + 30	▲	Alt + 226	Γ	Alt + 0193	Á	Alt + 0225	á
Alt + 4	♦	Alt + 31	▼	Alt + 235	δ	Alt + 0194	Â	Alt + 0226	â
Alt + 5	♣	**Line Arrows**		Alt + 238	ε	Alt + 0195	Ã	Alt + 0227	ã
Alt + 6	♠	Alt + 23	↕	Alt + 233	Θ	Alt + 0196	Ä	Alt + 0228	ä
Alt + 7	•	Alt + 24	↑	Alt + 227	π	Alt + 0197	Å	Alt + 0229	å
Alt + 8	◘	Alt + 25	↓	Alt + 228	Σ	Alt + 0198	Æ	Alt + 0230	æ
Alt + 9	○	Alt + 26	→	Alt + 229	σ	Alt + 0199	Ç	Alt + 0231	ç
Alt + 10	◙	Alt + 27	←	Alt + 231	τ	Alt + 0200	È	Alt + 0232	è
Alt + 11	♂	**Mathematical Symbols**		Alt + 232	Φ	Alt + 0201	É	Alt + 0233	é
Alt + 12	♀	Alt + 240	≡	Alt + 237	φ	Alt + 0202	Ê	Alt + 0234	ê
Alt + 13	♪	Alt + 241	±	Alt + 234	Ω	Alt + 0203	Ë	Alt + 0235	ë
Alt + 14	♫	Alt + 242	≥	**Authoring Symbols**		Alt + 0204	Ì	Alt + 0236	ì
Alt + 15	☼	Alt + 243	≤	Alt + 0153	™	Alt + 0205	Í	Alt + 0237	í
Editing		Alt + 247	≈	Alt + 0169	©	Alt + 0206	Î	Alt + 0238	î
Alt + 20	¶	Alt + 0137	‰	Alt + 0174	®	Alt + 0207	Ï	Alt + 0239	ï
Alt + 21	§	Alt + 0188	¼	**Currency**		Alt + 0209	Ñ	Alt + 0241	ñ
Alt + 28	∟	Alt + 0189	½	Alt + 155	¢	Alt + 0210	Ò	Alt + 0242	ò
Alt + 0134	†	Alt + 0190	¾	Alt + 156	£	Alt + 0211	Ó	Alt + 0243	ó
Alt + 0135	‡	Alt + 251	√	Alt + 157	¥	Alt + 0212	Ô	Alt + 0244	ô
Note: the code will not		Alt + 252	ⁿ	Alt + 158	₧	Alt + 0213	Õ	Alt + 0245	õ
appear until you		Alt + 0185	¹	Alt + 159	ƒ	Alt + 0214	Ö	Alt + 0246	ö
release the Alt key		Alt + 0178	²	Alt + 0128	€	Alt + 0217	Ù	Alt + 0249	ù
		Alt + 0179	³	**Special Punctuation**		Alt + 0218	Ú	Alt + 0250	ú
		Alt + 236	∞	Alt + 173	¡	Alt + 0219	Û	Alt + 0251	û
Note: to insert more		Alt + 230	µ	Alt + 168	¿	Alt + 0220	Ü	Alt + 0252	ü
exotic characters in		Alt + 228	Σ			Alt + 0221	Ý	Alt + 0253	ý
Word use the Insert		Alt + 239	∩			Alt + 0159	Ÿ	Alt + 0255	ÿ
menu, Symbol		Alt + 166	ª			Alt + 0142	Ž	Alt + 0142	Ž
command.		Alt + 167	º						

Drawing Icons									
Alt + 176	░	Alt + 186	║	Alt + 196	─	Alt + 206	╬	Alt + 215	╫
Alt + 177	▒	Alt + 187	╗	Alt + 197	┼	Alt + 207	╧	Alt + 216	╪
Alt + 178	▓	Alt + 188	╝	Alt + 198	╞	Alt + 208	╨	Alt + 217	┘
Alt + 179	│	Alt + 189	╜	Alt + 199	╟	Alt + 209	╤	Alt + 218	┌
Alt + 180	┤	Alt + 190	╛	Alt + 200	╚	Alt + 210	╥	Alt + 219	█
Alt + 181	╡	Alt + 191	┐	Alt + 201	╔	Alt + 211	╙	Alt + 220	▄
Alt + 182	╢	Alt + 192	└	Alt + 202	╩	Alt + 212	╘	Alt + 221	▌
Alt + 183	╖	Alt + 193	┴	Alt + 203	╦	Alt + 213	╒	Alt + 222	▐
Alt + 184	╕	Alt + 194	┬	Alt + 204	╠	Alt + 214	╓	Alt + 223	▀
Alt + 185	╣	Alt + 195	├	Alt + 205	═				

Prepared by Diane McKeever	www.100computertipsin100days.blogspot.com

Special Characters for Apple

Special Character Reference Sheet (for Apple computers)

Letters with Accents* see note below

ACCENT	SAMPLE	KEYS
Acute	ó Ó	Option+e
Circumflex	ô Ô	Option+i
Grave	ò Ò	Option+`
Tilde	õ Õ	Option+n
Umlaut	ö Ö	Option+u

Foreign Characters

SYMBOL	KEYS
¡	Option+1
¿	Shift+Option+?
Ç,ç	Shift+Option+C
	Option+C
Œ,œ	Shift+Option+Q
	Option+Q
ß	Option+S
º ª	Option+0
	Option+9
Ø,ø	Shift+Option+O
	Option+O
Å,å	Shift+Option+A
	Option+A
Æ,æ	Shift+Option+' (apostrophe)
	Option+'
« »	Option+\
	Shift+Option+\

Currency

SYMBOL	KEYS
¢	Option+4
£	Option+3
¥	Option+Y
€	Shift+Option+2
	May not be in older fonts.
ƒ	Option+F

Special Characters

SYMBOL	KEYS
©	Option+G
®	Option+R
™	Option+2
¶	Option+7
•	Option+8
§	Option+6
–	Option+-
—	Shift+Option+-
†	Option+T

Math Symbols

SYMBOL	KEYS
÷	Option+/
±	Shift+Option+=
°	Shift+Option+8
¬	Option+L
≥	Option+>
≤	Option+<
√	Option+V
π	Option+P
∞	Option+5
≈	Option+X
Δ	Option+J
Σ	Option+W
∏	Shift+Option+P
Ω	Option+Z
µ	Option+M
∂	Option+D
∫	Option+B
‰	Shift+Option+R

Note
*Hold down option key and type letter.
Release the option and type a vowel or Shift
and vowel for upper case.

**For accents on iPad/iPhone, hold down the letter key
and a menu of accent choices will appear**

Prepared by Diane McKeever
www.100computertipsin100days.blogspot.com

KEYBOARD SHORTCUTS FOR APPLE USERS

What it does	Key or key combination
Turn off your Mac or put it to sleep	Power button
Force your Mac to shut down	Hold down the power button
Force your Mac to restart	Command-Control-power button
Show restart/sleep/shutdown dialog	Control-Media Eject (⏏)
Put the computer to sleep	Command-Option-Media Eject (⏏)
Quit all applications (after giving you a chance to save changes to open documents), then restart the computer	Command-Control-Media Eject (⏏)
Quit all applications (after giving you a chance to save changes to open documents), then shut down the computer	Command-Option-Control-Media Eject (⏏)
Put all displays to sleep	Shift-Control-Media Eject (⏏)
Open desktop folder	Command-Shift-D
Eject	Command-E
Navigate to the search field in an already-open Spotlight window	Command-Option-F
Go to Folder	Command-Shift-G
Open the Home folder of the currently logged-in user account	Command-Shift-H
Get Info	Command-I
Show Inspector	Command-Option-I
Get Summary Info	Command-Control-I
Show View Options	Command-J
Minimize window	Command-M
Minimize all windows	Command-Option-M
New Finder window	Command-N
New folder	Command-Shift-N
New Smart Folder	Command-Option-N
Open selected item	Command-O
Log Out	Command-Shift-Q
Log Out immediately	Command-Shift-Option-Q
Show original (of alias)	Command-R

Add to Sidebar	Command-T
Add to Favorites	Command-Shift-T
Hide Toolbar / Show Toolbar in Finder windows	Command-Option-T
Open Utilities folder	Command-Shift-U
Paste	Command-V
Close window	Command-W
Close all windows	Command-Option-W
Cut	Command-X
Slideshow (Mac OS X v10.5 or later)	Command-Option-Y
Undo / Redo	Command-Z
View as Icon	Command-1
View as List	Command-2
View as Columns	Command-3
View as Cover Flow (Mac OS X v10.5 or later)	Command-4
Open Finder preferences	Command-Comma (,)
Cycle through open Finder windows	Command-Accent (`) (the Accent key above Tab key on a US English keyboard layout)
Open Mac Help	Command-Shift-Question Mark (?)
Go to the previous folder	Command-Left Bracket ([)
Go to the next folder	Command-Right Bracket (])
Open the folder that contains the current folder	Command-Up Arrow
Open the folder that contains the current folder in a new window	Command-Control-Up Arrow
Open highlighted item	Command-Down Arrow
Make the desktop active	Command-Shift-Up Arrow
Open the selected folder	Right Arrow (in List view)
Close the selected folder	Left Arrow (in List view)
Open all folders within the selected folder	Option-click the disclosure triangle (in List view)
Open a folder in a separate window, closing the current window	Option–double-click

Open a folder in a separate window	Command–double-click
See the folders that contain the current window	Command-click the window title
Switch application–cycle forward	Command-Tab
Switch application–cycle backward	Command-Shift-Tab
Move to Trash	Command-Delete
Empty Trash	Command-Shift-Delete
Empty Trash without confirmation dialog	Command-Shift-Option-Delete
Quick Look (Mac OS X v10.5 or later)	Space bar (or Command-Y)
Move dragged item to other volume/location (pointer icon changes while key is held)	Command key while dragging
Copy dragged item (pointer icon changes while key is held)	Option key while dragging
Make alias of dragged item (pointer icon changes while key is held)	Command-Option key combination while dragging

QUICK REFERENCE GUIDES

The following Quick Reference tip cards can be printed for handy reference.
All the guides are designed to be printed two sided.

Office 2010
QUICK REFERENCE GUIDE

www.dianemckeever.com

THE RIBBON

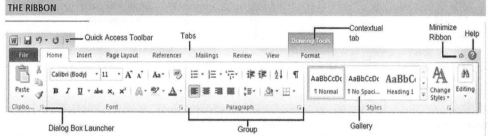

Ribbon: Displays the commands and tools you need to perform various tasks. The Ribbon can also be minimized and customized to fit your work style

Tabs: Display the commands you can use in a Microsoft Office program. Click a tab to view its commands.

Contextual Tabs: display commands for a selected object.

Dialog Box Launcher: Click to open a dialog box or task pane.

Group: Related commands that appear under each tab.

Gallery: A list of options and additional choices displayed as thumbnail previews so you can see results before making choices.

Quick Access Toolbar: Provides quick access to the commands you use most frequently. The Save, Undo, and Redo/Repeat buttons appear on the Quick Access Toolbar by default.

To Minimize the Ribbon: Click the Minimize Ribbon button on the Ribbon or double-click a tab on the.

To Customize the Ribbon: right-click a tab and select Customize the Ribbon from the menu or click the File tab, select Options and click the Customize Ribbon command. Use the controls in the dialog box to rename and rearrange tabs and to rearrange tab commands.

- Click the **New Tab** button to create a new tab on the Ribbon
- Click the **New Group** button to create a new group in a tab on the Ribbon

To Add a Command to the Quick Access Toolbar: Click the Customize Quick Access Toolbar button and select a command from the menu. Click More Commands to select from a longer list of commands.

Get Help: Click the Help button or press F1 or, click the File tab and select Help from the menu.

FILE TAB AND BACKSTAGE VIEW AND COMMANDS

Info: Set permissions to control who can open or change the document; prepare the file for sharing by removing metadata and other personal information; and view and manage Autosaved versions of the document.

Recent: Displays documents most recently opened in the program. Use the push pin to anchor the documents to the list.

New: Create a new blank document or create a document from a template. Browse templates with the preview feature in Backstage view.

Print: Preview the document and select print settings at the same time. The right pane displays a preview of the file, the center pane displays print options.

Share: Share the file and change file type. There are four ways to share a document:

1. **Send Using E-mail**: Send the document as an attachment, a link, a PDF or XPS, or fax.
2. **Save to SkyDrive**: Save to a SkyDrive folder through your Windows Live account.
3. **Save to SharePoint**: Saves to a SharePoint workspace on your computer.
4. **Publish**: Publish the document to a service or blog.

QUICK TIP

The File tab replaces the File menu and Office Button found in previous versions of Microsoft Office. Common file management commands (Save, Save As, Open and Close) appear at the top of the menu. Backstage view appears when you click the File tab. The left panel displays commands in the file tab menu. The center panel displays options related to the selected command. The right panel displays a preview or additional options for a command.

INSERT SMARTART

To Insert SmartArt: Click the Insert tab on the Ribbon and click the SmartArt option in the Illustrations group. Choose the category of SmartArt and then the type from the list. Use the Type your text here area to insert text in the SmartArt.

PICTURE TOOLS

To Remove Backgrounds: Click the Format tab on the ribbon and click the Remove Background option in the Adjust group. Refine the image and click Keep Changes

To Correct Brightness and Contrast or to Sharpen or Soften a Picture: Click the Format tab on the Ribbon, click the Corrections option in the Adjust group and select an option from the Gallery.

To Change the color of a Picture: Click the Format tab on the Ribbon, click the Color option in the Adjust group and select an option from the gallery

To Apply an Artistic Effect: Click the Format tab on the Ribbon, click the Artistic Effects option in the Adjust group and select an option from the gallery.

WORD ART

WordArt has received a huge face life in Office 2010. New WordArt styles and functionality make it easy to add and format WordArt. It is also treated as text instead of a picture, so the text is now searchable in the document.

To Add WordArt: Click the Insert tab on the ribbon and click the WordArt option in the Text group. Select a WordArt style and type the text in the text box.

To Move WordArt: Click the WordArt object, drag it to the desired location and release the mouse button

To Format WordArt. Click the WordArt object, then click the Format tab on the Ribbon under drawing tools. Select a formatting option in the WordArt Styles group or select a new WordArt style from the gallery.

FILE MANAGEMENT TOOLS

Office 2010 offers new and improved tools to help you manage, protect and share your content.

Autosaved Versions: This feature improves on the AutoRecover feature from earlier versions of Office. The AutoRecover feature automatically saves versions of your files at regular intervals. Now you can access those versions whenever you want. This makes it easy to revert to an earlier version of the file or to recover charges when you forget to save manually.

To Recover Autosaved Versions: Click the File tab on the Ribbon and select info. Select an Autosaved version from the Versions list. Or, click the Manage Versions button and select Recover Draft Versions.

Protected view: Protected view protects you from cyber-attacks by opening the file as read-only. When a file appears to be from a risky location, such as the Internet, it is opened in Protected view. If you trust the file, you can enable editing and work with the file as usual.

Trusted documents: Trusted documents now remembers the trust decisions you make in a document so you don't have to be asked if a document with active content (e.g. Macros, ActiveX controls, etc.) is safe every time you open it.

To Use the Accessibility Checker: Click the File tab on the ribbon and select Info. Click the Check for issues option and select Check Accessibility.

CAPTURING SCREENSHOTS

To Insert a Screenshot: click the Insert tab on the Ribbon and click the Screenshot option in the Illustrations group (Word/Excel/Outlook) or the Images group (PowerPoint), then click an available window.

To Insert a Screen Clipping: click the Insert tab on the Ribbon and click the Screenshot option in the Illustrations group (Word/Excel/Outlook) or the Images group (PowerPoint), then click Screen Clipping. Click and drag your mouse across the area of the program window that you want to clip.

Word 2010
QUICK REFERENCE GUIDE

www.dianemckeever.com

THE WORD 2010 SCREEN

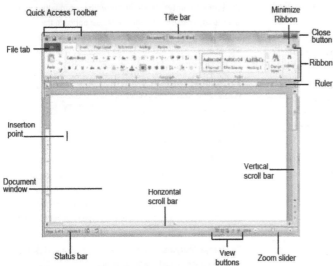

Quick Access Toolbar

Title bar

Minimize Ribbon

Close button

File tab

Ribbon

Ruler

Insertion point

Vertical scroll bar

Document window

Horizontal scroll bar

Status bar

View buttons

Zoom slider

KEYBOARD SHORTCUTS	
GENERAL	
New Document	Ctrl + n
Open Document	Ctrl + o
Save Document	Ctrl + s
Print Document	Ctrl + p
Quit Program	Ctrl + w
Help	F1
NAVIGATION	
Up one Screen	Page Up
Down one Screen	Page Down
Beginning of Line	Home
End of Line	End
Beginning of document	Ctrl + Home
End of document	Ctrl + End
EDITING	
Undo	Ctrl + z
Cut	Ctrl + x
Copy	Ctrl + c
Paste	Ctrl + v
SELECTING TEXT	
Word	Dbl click the word
Paragraph	Triple click the paragraph
Sentence	Ctrl click the sentence
Whole document	Ctrl + a
Variable	Click at the beginning of text, hold down the Shift key and click at the end of the text.

FILE TAB AND BACKSTAGE VIEW AND COMMANDS

To Create a New Document: Click the File tab, click the New option and click the Create button.

To Open a Document: Click the File tab and click the Open option.

To Save a Document: Click the Save button on the Quick Access Toolbar.

To Save a Document with a Different Name or File type: Click the File tab, click the Save As option and enter a new name or select a different file type for the document.

To Preview and Print Document: Click the File tab and click the Print option.

To Undo: Click the Undo button on the Quick Access Toolbar.

To Move Text with the Mouse: Select the text you want to move. Position your mouse on the selected text, hold down the mouse button and drag to a new location. Release the mouse button.

To Move Text with the Menus: Select the text you want to move. From the Home tab, Clipboard group choose Cut. Click where you want the text moved to and choose Paste from the Home tab, Clipboard group.

To Replace Text: Click the Replace option in the Editing group on the Home tab.

To Close a Document: Click Close "X" on the window.

To Correct a Spelling, Grammar or Homophone Errors: Right-click the error and select a correction from the contextual menu.

To Minimize the Ribbon: Click the Minimize Ribbon option on the Ribbon, or double-click the tab.

To Change Program Settings: Click the File tab and click the Options button

To Get Help: Press F! to open the Help window or click the blue help question mark button.

236

EDITING

To Cut or Copy Text: Select the text you want to cut or copy and click the Cut or Copy option in the Clipboard group on the Home tab.

To Paste Text: Place the insertion point where you want to paste and click the Paste option in the Clipboard group on the Home tab

To Preview an Item Before Pasting: Place the insertion point where you want to paste, click the Paste option list arrow in the Clipboard group on the Home tab and select a preview option to view the item.

To Insert a Comment: Select the text where you want to insert a comment and click the Review tab. Click the New Comment option in the Comments group. Type a comment, then click outside the comment text box.

To Delete a Comment: Select the comment, click the Review tab and click the Delete Comment option in the Comments group.

TABLES

To Insert a Table: Click the Insert tab, click the Table option in the Tables group and select Insert Table from the list.

To Insert a Column or Row: Click the Layout tab under the Table Tools and use the commands located in the Rows & Columns group.

To Delete a Column or Row: Select the column or row you want to delete. Click the Layout tab under Table Tools and click the Delete button in the Rows & Columns group. Make an appropriate selection from the list.

To Adjust Column Width or Row Height: Position your mouse on the vertical or horizontal line you want to adjust. Hold down the mouse button and move the mouse left/right or up/down. This can also be adjusted using the Layout tab, Cell Size group. Choosing the Auto Fit option will automatically adjust the column

TRACKING CHANGES

To Turn on Tracking: Click the Track Changes option in the Tracking group on the Review tab. As you make editing changes to the document they will be shown along with the original text. Each person who makes a change will automatically have a different color assigned.

On the Insert tab, the ~~fabulous~~ galleries look of ~~your~~ our document. You can use pages, and other document building blo

To Identify Change User Information: Hover on the changed text and a box will appear identify the user and the date and time of the change.

To Accept/Reject Changes: Use the Accept/Reject options in the Changes group on the Review tab.

FORMATTING

To Format Text: Use the commands in the Font group on the Home tab.

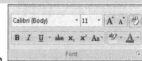

To Copy Formatting with the Format Painter: Select the text with the formatting you want to copy and click the Format Painter option in the Clipboard group on the Home tab. Click once for one use and twice for unlimited uses. Then select the text to which you want to apply the copied formatting.

To Indent a Paragraph: Click the Increase Indent button in the Paragraph group on the Home tab

To Decrease an Indent: Click the Decrease Indent button in the Paragraph group on the Home tab.

To Create a Bulleted or Numbered List: Select the paragraphs you want to bullet or number and click the Bullets or Numbering option in the Paragraph group on the Home tab. Use the Bullets or Numbering option list arrow to view type of bullets or numbering schemes.

To Change Margins: Click the Page Layout tab and click the Margins option in the Page Setup group.

To Change Page Orientation: Click the Page Layout tab and click the Orientation option in the Page Setup group.

To Insert a Header or Footer: Click the Insert tab and click the Header or Footer option in the Header & Footer group.

To Insert a Manual Page Break: Click the Insert tab and click the Page Break button in the Pages group.

DRAWING AND GRAPHICS

To Insert Clip Art: Click the Insert tab and click the Clip Art option in the Illustrations group. Type the name of what you're looking for in the "Search for" box and press Enter. Click o Clip Art to add to the document.

To Insert a Picture: Click the Insert tab and click the Picture button in the Illustrations group. Find and select the picture you want to insert and click Insert.

To Insert WordArt: Click the Insert tab, click the WordArt button in the Text group and select a design from the WordArt Gallery. Click the text box and enter your text. If necessary, click the text box and drag it to the desired position.

To Insert SmartArt: Click the Insert tab, click the SmartArt button in the Illustrations group, select a layout and click OK.

To Resize an Object: Click the object, click and drag one of its sizing handles. Use corner resize handles to keep it in proportion while resizing it.

To Delete an Object: Select the object and press the Delete key.

Excel 2010
QUICK REFERENCE GUIDE

www.dianemckeever.com

THE EXCEL 2010 SCREEN

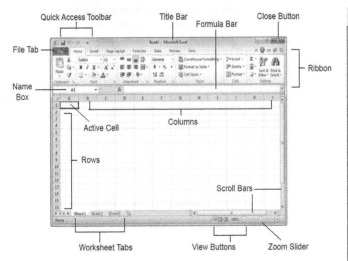

KEYBOARD SHORTCUTS

GENERAL

New Workbook	Ctrl + n
Open Workbook	Ctrl + o
Save Workbook	Ctrl + s
Preview & Print Workbook	Ctrl + p
Quit Program	Ctrl + w
Help	F1

NAVIGATION

Right One Cell	Tab
Down One Cell	Enter
Down One Screen	Page Down
Up One Screen	Page Up
To Cell A1	Ctrl + Home
To Last Cell	Ctrl + End

EDITING

Undo	Ctrl + z
Cut	Ctrl + x
Copy	Ctrl + c
Paste	Ctrl + v
Redo	Ctrl + y
Select All	Ctrl + a
Clear cell contents	Delete key

THE FUNDAMENTALS

To Create a New Workbook: Click the file tab, click the New option and click the Create button.

To Open a Workbook: Click the File tab and click the Open option.

To Save a Workbook: Click the Save button on the Quick Access Toolbar.

To Save a Workbook with a Different Name or File type: Click the File tab, click the Save As button and enter a new name or select a different file type for the document.

To Preview and Print Workbook: click the File tab and click the Print option.

To Undo: Click the Undo button on the Quick Access Toolbar.

To Close a Workbook: Click Close "X" on the window or choose Close from the File tab.

To Minimize the Ribbon: Click the Minimize Ribbon option on the Ribbon, or double-click the tab.

To Get Help: Press F1 to open the Help window or click the blue help question mark button.

Cell Addresses: Cells are referenced by addresses made from their column letter and row number, such as cell A1, A2, B3, etc. You can find the address of a cell by looking at the Name Box.

To Select a Cell: Click a cell or use the keyboard arrow keys to select it.

To Select a Cell Range: Click the first cell, hold down the Shift key and click the last cell.

To Select an Entire Worksheet: Ctrl + a

To Use Zoom: Click and drag the zoom slider to the left or right.

To Customize the Ribbon: Right-click any tab and select Customize the Ribbon from the menu or click the File tab, select Options and click the Customize Ribbon command. Use the controls in the dialog box to rename and rearrange tabs and to rearrange tab commands.

- Click the **New Tab** button to create a new tab on the Ribbon.

- Click the **New Group** button to create a new group in a tab on the Ribbon.

OPERATORS

Operators Used In Formulas/Functions:

Addition:	+ (plus)
Subtraction	— (minus)
Multiplication	* (star)
Division	/ (slash)
Operation Order	( ) (parenthesis)

Used to group operations. For example:

=(A1*G27)/3

A1 would be multiplied by G27 and the result of that would be divided by 3

EDITING

To Edit a Cell's Contents: Select the cell and click the Formula Bar, or double-click the cell. Edit the cell contents and press the Enter key.

To Preview an Item Before Pasting: Place the insertion point where you want to paste, click the Paste button list arrow in the Clipboard group on the Home tab, and select a preview option.

To Copy Using Auto Fill: Point to the fill handle at the bottom-right corner of the selected cell(s), then drag to the destination cell(s).

To Complete a Series Using AutoFill: Select the cells that define the series. Click and drag the fill handle to complete the series.

To Insert a Column or Row: Right-click to the right of the column, or below the row you want to insert. Select Insert from the contextual menu, or click the Insert button in the Cells group on the Home tab.

To Delete a Column or Row: Select the row or column heading(s). Right-click and select Delete from the contextual menu, or click the Delete button in the Cells group on the Home tab.

To Insert a Comment: Select the cell where you want to insert a comment and click the Review tab on the Ribbon. Click the New Comment button in the Comments group. Type a comment and click outside the comment box.

FORMULAS AND FUNCTIONS

To Total a Cell Range: Click the cell where you want to insert the total and click the Sum button in the Editing group on the Home tab. Verify the selected cell range and click the Sum button again or press the Enter key.

To Enter a Formula: Select the cell where you want to insert the formula. Type an equal sign (=) and enter the formula using values, cell references, operators and functions. Press the Enter key when you're finished.

To Insert a Function: Select the cell where you want to enter the function and click the Insert Function button on the Formula Bar or select from a function group.

To Reference a Cell in a Formula: Type the cell reference in the formula or click on a cell.

To Create an Absolute Cell Reference: Precede the cell references with a $ sign. Use the F4 key to add $ signs.

To Use Several Operators or Cell Ranges: Enclose the part of a formula you want to calculate first in parentheses.

DATA ACTIONS

To Sort Data: Select a cell in the column to be sorted and click Sort & Filter in the Editing group on the Home tab.

To Filter Data: Click the Sort & Filter command in the Editing group on the Home tab. Pull down menus will allow you to filter the data.

FORMATTING

To Format Text: Use the commands in the Font group on the Home tab.

To Format Values: Use the commands in the Number group on the Home tab.

To copy Formatting with the Format Painter: Select the cell(s) with the formatting you want to copy and click the Format Painter option in the Clipboard group on the Home tab. Click it once for one use, twice for unlimited uses. Then, select the cell(s) you want to apply the copied formatting to.

To Apply a Cell Style: Select the cell(s) you want to apply a cell style to. Click the Cell Styles button in the Styles group of the Home tab and select a style from the gallery.

To Apply Conditional Formatting: Select the cells to which you want to apply conditional formatting. Click the Conditional Formatting button in the Styles group of the Home tab. Select the formatting scheme you wish to use, then set the conditions in the dialog box.

To Adjust Column Width or Row Height. Drag the right border of the column header or the bottom border of the row header. Double-click the border to AutoFit the column or row according to its contents.

CHARTS

To Create a Chart: Select the cell range that contains the data you want to chart and press the F11 key. The chart is inserted in a new sheet in the book.

To Insert a Sparkline: Select the cell range that contains the data you want to chart and click the Insert tab. Select the sparkline you want to insert from the Sparkline group. Select the cell or cell range where you want to add the sparkline and click

WORKBOOK MANAGEMENT

To Insert a New Worksheet: Click the Insert Worksheet tab to the right of the last sheet tab.

To Delete a Worksheet: Right-click the sheet tab and select Delete from the contextual menu.

To Rename a Worksheet: Double-click the sheet tab, enter a new name and press the Enter key.

To Change a Worksheet's Tab Color: Right-click the sheet tab, select Tab Color and choose the color to apply.

To Move a Worksheet: Click and drag the worksheet tab.

To Copy a Worksheet: Hold down the Ctrl key while dragging the sheet tab.

To Protect or Share a Workbook: Click the Review tab on the Ribbon and use the commands in the Changes group.

To Recover Autosaved Versions: Click the File tab and select Info. Select an autosaved version from the Versions list. Or, click the Manage Versions button and select Recover Draft Versions.

Questions? Email Diane: diane@dianemckeever.com

Outlook 2010

QUICK REFERENCE GUIDE

www.dianemckeever.com

THE OUTLOOK 2010 SCREEN

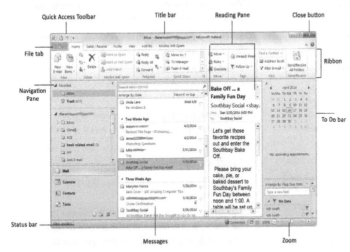

Quick Access Toolbar — Title bar — Reading Pane — Close button

File tab

Navigation Pane

Ribbon

To Do bar

Status bar

Messages — Zoom

THE FUNDAMENTALS

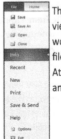

The File tab and Backstage view contain commands for working with a program's files such as Save As, Save Attachments, Close, New and Print.

To Check for New Messages: Click the Send/Receive All Folders option.

To Preview and Print a Message: Click the file tab and select Print.

To Minimize the Ribbon: Right-click a tab and select Minimize Ribbon from the contextual menu.

To Get Help: Press F1 to open the Help window. Type your question and press Enter.

QUICK STEPS

This new feature in Outlook 2010 enables you to quick perform frequent actions such as sending an e-mail to your supervisor or your team.

NAVIGATION PANE

Mail Contains mail-related folders like your Inbox, Sent Items, and Search Folders. Use the Favorites section at the top of the pane for easy access to frequently used folders.

Calendar Lets you view and schedule appointments, events and meetings. View shared calendars and compare calendars by viewing them side-by-side.

Tasks Organize to-do lists, track task progress and delegate tasks.

Notes Use like electronic Post-It® Notes to write down information.

Contacts Store contact information including addresses, phone numbers and e-mail addresses.

MAIL: BASICS

To Create a New Message::

1. Click the New E-mail option in the New group of the Home tab.
2. Enter the e-mail address(es) in the To: CC: or BCC: boxes
3. Enter the Subject of the message in the Subject box.
4. Enter the text of your message in the text box.
5. Click the Send button.

To Reply to a Message: Select/open the message, click the Reply option, type your reply and click the Send button.

To Forward a Message: Select/open the message, click the Forward option, enter the

e-mail address(es), enter comments in the Body area, and click the Send button.

To Delete a Message: Select the message and press the Delete key. To permanently delete a message hold down the Shift key and then press the Delete key.

To Open a Message: Click a message to view it in the Reading Pane or double-click the message to open it.

Message Indicators:

📩 Unread message

✉ Read message

📎 Message with an attachment

❗ Message that has high importance

KEYBOARD SHORTCUTS

New Item	Ctrl + n
Send	Ctrl + Enter
Save	Ctrl + s
Preview and Print	Ctrl + p
Undo	Ctrl + z
Cut	Ctrl + x
Copy	Ctrl + c
Paste	Ctrl + v
Check Spelling	F7
Check for Mail	F9
Reply	Ctrl + r
Reply to All	Alt + l
Help	F1

MAIL: ADVANCED TASKS

To Attach a File to a Message: Click the Attach Item command in the Include group of the Message tab in the Message window.

To Preview an Attachment: Click the attachment in the message preview in the Reading Pane.

To Open an Attachment: Double-click the attachment in the Reading Pane.

To Flag a Message as a To-Do Item: Right-click the message and select Follow Up from the contextual menu. Select a flag.

To Categorize a Message by Color: Click the Quick Click icon on the message.

To Resend a Message: Open the Sent Items folder. Double-click the message, click the Actions option in the Move group of the Message tab. Select Resend This Message. Edit the message and recipients as necessary and click Send.

To Create a Signature: In the message window, click the Signature option in the Include group of the Message tab. Select Signatures and create a new signature. Create a signature to use when replying.

To Change a Message's Options: In the message window, click the Options tab. Here you can specify the importance of the message, add voting buttons, direct where replies should be sent, request a read receipt and if you want to encrypt the message or delay its delivery.

To Create a Folder: Right-click the Inbox folder and from the contextual menu choose New Folder. Name the folder and click OK.

To Move a Message to a Different Folder: Select the item, click the Move button in the Move group of the Home tab, and then select the destination folder. Or, click and drag the item to a different folder in the Navigation Pane.

To Turn On the Out of Office Assistant: Click the File tab, select Info, and click the Automatic Replies option.

To Create a New Rule: Click the Rules button in the Move group of the Home tab and select Create Rule.

To Manage Rules: Click the Rules button in the Move group of the Home tab and select Manage Rules and Alerts.

TASKS AND TO-DO ITEMS

To Open Tasks/To-Lo List: Click the Tasks option in the Navigation Pane and select To-Do List or Tasks in the Navigation Pane.

To Create a New Task/To-Do Item: Click the New Task button in the New group on the Home tab.

To Complete a Task: Click the Mark Complete button in the Manage Task group on the Ribbon, or click the task's check box in Simple List view.

To Delete a Task: Select the task and press the Delete key. Or, click the Delete button in the Delete group of the Home tab.

CALENDAR

To Open the Calendar: Click the Calendar button in the Navigation Pane.

To Change Views: Click a view option in the Arrange group on the Home tab, or click the View tab and select an option there.

To View a Specific Date: Click the date in the Date Navigator, or click and drag to view a set of consecutive dates.

To Schedule an Appointment: Click the New Appointment button in the New group on the Home tab.

To Schedule a Recurring Appointment: Click the New Items option in the New group. Select More Items, Recurring Appointment.

To Schedule a Meeting: Click the New Meeting option in the New group. Add recipients and meeting details and click Send.

To Schedule an All Day Event: Click the New Items button in the New group and select All Day Event.

To Reschedule an Item: Click and drag the item to a new date and/or time on the Calendar.

To Edit an Item: Click the item to view the calendar Tools contextual tab. Or, double-click the item, make your changes, and click the Save & Close button in the Actions group on the Ribbon.

To Delete an item: Select the item and press the Delete key.

To Search the Calendar: Click in the Search box in the upper right corner. Type the search keywords and press the Enter key.

CONTACTS

To Open Contacts: Click the Contacts button in the Navigation Pane.

To Change Views: click a view option in the Arrange group on the Home tab or click the View tab and select an option there.

To create a New Contact: Click the New Contact button in the New group on the Home tab. Or right-click on a message received from this person and choose Add to Contacts.

To Create a New Contact Group: Click the New Contact Group option in the New group of the Home tab Click the Add Members button in the Members group on the Ribbon, select a name in the list, click the Members button and repeat for each name to be added. Click OK, then click Save & Close in the Actions group of the Contact Group tab.

To Edit a Contact: Double-click the contact and make your changes. Click Save & Close.

To Find a Contact: Typ0e your search text in the Search Contacts field. Or, click the Find a Contact field in the Find group on the Home tab, enter your search text and press the Enter key.

CPSIA information can be obtained at www.ICGtesting.com
Printed in the USA
LVOW03s0100041014

407236LV00002B/3/P